PRINCIPIA SCRIPTORIAE *with*
BETWEEN EAST AND WEST

Richard Nelson's plays include *Two Shakespearean Actors* (Lincoln Center Theater in New York, Royal Shakespeare Company in Stratford-upon-Avon and London), *Some Americans Abroad* (Lincoln Center, RSC), *Sensibility and Sense* (American Playhouse Television), *The Return of Pinocchio*, *Rip Van Winkle or The Works*, *The Vienna Notes*, and *An American Comedy*. He is also the author of the book for the Broadway musical *Chess* and the adaptor of Beaumarchais's *The Marriage of Figaro* and Dario Fo's *Accidental Death of an Anarchist* (both Broadway). His plays for television and radio include *The End of a Sentence* (American Playhouse), *Advice to Eastern Europe* (BBC), *Eating Words* (BBC), *Roots in Water* (BBC), and *Languages Spoken Here* (BBC). His screenplay of Edith Wharton's *Ethan Frome* will be filmed in 1992.

Among Nelson's awards are the prestigious Lila Wallace–Reader's Digest Award in 1991, a London Time Out Award, two Obies, two Giles Cooper Awards, a Guggenheim fellowship, two Rockefeller playwriting grants and two National Endowment for the Arts playwriting fellowships.

Principia Scriptoriae received its first full production at the Manhattan Theatre Club in 1986. The first full production of *Between East and West* was at the Yale Repertory Theatre in 1985.

by the same author

**SENSIBILITY AND SENSE
SOME AMERICANS ABROAD
TWO SHAKESPEAREAN ACTORS**

PRINCIPIA SCRIPTORIAE

with

BETWEEN EAST AND WEST

RICHARD NELSON

ff

Faber and Faber
BOSTON • LONDON

All rights reserved under International and Pan-American
Copyright Conventions, including the right of reproduction
in whole or in part in any form.
This collection first published in the United States
by Faber and Faber, Inc., 50 Cross Street, Winchester, MA 01890.
First published in Great Britain in 1991 by Faber and Faber Ltd,
3 Queen Square, London WC1N 3AU.

Principia Scriptoriae © 1986 by Richard Nelson
Between East and West © 1983, 1985, 1989 by Richard Nelson
Introduction © 1991 by Richard Nelson

Written permission is required for live performance of any sort.
This includes readings, cuttings, scenes, and excerpts.
For amateur and stock performances, please contact Broadway Play Publishing Inc.,
357 W. 20th Street, New York, NY 10011.
For all other rights, contact Peter Franklin, William Morris Agency,
1350 Sixth Avenue, New York, NY 10019.

This book is sold subject to the condition that it shall not,
by way of trade or otherwise, be lent, re-sold, hired out or otherwise
circulated without the publisher's prior consent in any form of binding
or cover other than that in which it is published and
without a similar condtion including this condition being imposed
on the subsequent purchaser.

Library of Congress Cataloging-in-Publication Data

Nelson, Richard, 1950–
  [Principia scriptoriae]
  Principia scriptoriae; with, Between East and West / Richard
Nelson.
    p. cm.
  ISBN 0-571-12905-6 : $12.95
  I. Nelson, Richard, 1950– Between East and West. II. Title.
III. Title: Between East and West.
PS3564.E4747P7 1992
812'.54—dc20   91-24735
                                                                          CIP

A CIP record for this book is
available from the British Library.

Printed in the United States of America

CONTENTS

Introduction by Richard Nelson   vii
Principia Scriptoriae   5
Between East and West   62

INTRODUCTION

I have long looked forward to this volume's publication, believing as I do that these two plays, which were written back-to-back between 1983 and 1985, complement each other, or perhaps are efforts to tell the same story. They represent an artistic watershed for me and show a growth over my previous plays, at least in terms of my craft. They are also the first of my plays to have been produced in London and are therefore responsible for precipitating the generous and invaluable relationship I now have with the theater of that city. Thirdly, I think they reflect a time in my life of great change and confusion. As such, I have a warm spot in my heart for what they attempted to do—not as plays, but as necessary expressions of my state of mind.

It is always a little reductionist to explain why one wrote a particular piece; so many things go into the mix, affecting everything else already in the mix, that it is slightly untruthful to point out two or three ingredients and call them the whole recipe. Given this disclaimer, or rather admission that I can be as untruthful about my work as others can, I have come to see in retrospect how three occurrences, each beginning in 1983, had a vital impact upon me, my work, and these two plays in particular.

In October 1983, my mother, aged 59, was diagnosed as having terminal lung cancer. Therein began the nightmare so many have gone through and so many will—her pain and treatment, fears and angers both hers and my father's. Having spent the better part of my last twenty-five years far away from the homes my parents moved to, I was not very well-prepared to play the part of son—the role I now very much needed to fill, both for my parents' sake and for mine.

In December 1983, halfway between the diagnosis and my mother's death, my first child, Zoe was born. The joy of this I simply was not prepared for either; feelings unknown to me just burst forth unannounced. Just as I was struggling to be a son, I was suddenly struggling equally hard to be a father.

The third occurrence was purely artistic. In November 1983, my friend, the director Livu Ciulei (then artistic director of the Guthrie Theater in Minneapolis) asked me to do a new translation (or English version based on a literal translation, as I know no Russian) of Chekhov's *Three Sisters* for the Guthrie. I much admired Chekhov's plays, of course, though until then I had seen them more as an influence on softer, more atmospheric writers than on the ironic and social playwrights I wished to emulate. But in doing this translation (and perhaps in doing it at this emotionally vivid time in my life where ambiguity seemed to me the very essence of life), I realized how I had misread this great writer; instead of "atmosphere" and blurred edges and melancholia, what I found in Chekhov was a voice pulsing with humor, irony, confusion, contradiction, and passion for life and for the pain of life. In other words, a voice for all I was suddenly feeling and trying to understand in myself and my life. Serendipity had made me focus on the one playwright whose world seemed best able to describe what I was now seeing in mine; it wasn't long before I realized that artistically too I was changing, or rather had no choice but to change.

These three events, then, literally blew me apart, or perhaps I should say, blew me open—emotionally, psychologically, physically and artistically. *Principia Scriptoriae* and *Between East and West* were my initial efforts to put the pieces back together.

Between East and West was suggested by the lives of an Eastern European middle-aged couple I'd first met in the 1970s and had gotten to know very well and to admire over the next years. He is a director and she a critic, and for a time they lived in a tiny, sparsely furnished apartment on New York's Upper East Side while he looked for work and she wanted to leave America. They were and are extraordinarily charming, interesting, full of passion for ideas, art, culture and politics; generous with their time and attentions. Irony was never far from the surface of either; they seemed to love and breathe an energy and focus that I wished to possess. I fell in love with both of them, and they eventually became for me surrogate parents of a sort. So it was upon them (with their permission) that I built.

In the play they became Czechoslovakian (they aren't), and she became an actress. The couple's relationship grew—in my mind—to encompass thoughts I was having about my parents' lives together and *their* various moves around the country (seven since I was a child), as well as what must have been my parents' feelings of exile and displacement, had they allowed such self-reflection to enter into their thinking. My mother had been a dancer when she was young and had given this up for marriage and family. With her children long since on their own, she found herself in her late fifties and in the middle of yet another move to another city. Then she was diagnosed as having terminal cancer. She must have felt completely in between everything, unable to find any firm earth under her feet. During our hours and hours of talks while she was dying, I sensed in her a feeling of great loss, a loneliness for a life spent in some sort of exile, where "home" never materialized for her.

At this same time in my own energized state of trying to be son/father, I no doubt was very ripe for just such feelings. Given that politically I remained an unrepentant product of the 1960s, a very great sin in 1983, my own feelings of being in exile or at least estranged (in my case, from my country) thrived as well. Add to this my position as a writer with a string of critically unsuccessful plays behind me (plays which, though perhaps flawed, attempted to address a world in terms of some variety and complexity). I was ready to sympathize with anyone feeling neglected, rejected, and—especially given the changing nature of my life—*between things*.

All of this, I suppose now, was inside me as I sat down to write *Between East and West*, which I would have called *Home* had not David Storey already written a very good play by that title. I wrote the play in fragments, then attempted to find a narrative voice that would leave room in the work for both the realism of the fragments and the point of view of the storyteller. I was hoping to create for an audience an experience where real involvement in the moment of a scene was followed by withdrawal from that involvement, then back again. This, if I remember my intention correctly, might let an audience into the world I most wished it to experience—that of "betweenness."

The play was first performed in a workshop production in

Seattle. There were only two weeks of rehearsal. Normally I would not have agreed to such a production: any new play certainly needs more than two weeks and anything less risks the play's being criticized unfairly. However, this production paid for me, my wife and daughter to fly the three thousand miles to the West Coast, where my parents lived; and so we were all able to see my mother this one extra time before she died.

The production was a mess by the time I arrived (halfway through the two weeks); stage directions, sparsely written, had been ignored and confusion reigned — the kitchen, where a number of scenes take place, could not be seen by half of the audience, so the kitchen scenes were being staged in the dining room and I was now being told that some of my dialogue and business would have to be rewritten to fit this change. I was also told by one of the actors that a great deal of energy had gone into efforts to "act Czech," whatever this means. So instead of this being my chance to see where my changing artistic and emotional self was headed or what it had already achieved, this first production was more an effort to get something up that was not embarrassing.

I next heard the play that summer near my home in a small summer theater in Woodstock, New York. The producer of the theater had asked to have the reading (for a very small, invited and, thank God, non-paying audience), using friends of his, two emigré Polish actors. They read brilliantly (and reignited my enthusiasms after Seattle) and seemed to understand the work perfectly, even profoundly, from their own experiences. But when I was asked if a full production could be mounted with these two wonderful actors I had to say no: because of the device of the play (when speaking Czech the characters use accents, when not, not), two very accented Poles would be too confusing. The bitter irony of my decision, given the play's plot and concerns, was not lost on me.

Next were full productions at Yale Repertory Theatre in New Haven, Connecticut, and Hampstead Theatre Club in London, directed by John Madden and David Jones respectively. Both productions found the play I hoped I'd written; the first built off the play's melancholy, the latter on its sense of loss and frustration. In both, I thought I saw and heard my Eastern European friends, my mother and father, and my sadness about my country. In the productions' structure, at times I could also hear that person trying so hard to put to order these feelings of exile and loneliness and loss of home. That person, of course, being me.

There are bad titles for plays that are bad because they don't relate to the play they're naming, or because they are boring or trite or just bland. And then, more rarely, there are titles that are bad simply because no one knows how to say them and so to avoid embarrassment they avoid trying. This is the case, I fear, with *Principia Scriptoriae*, which, to this day, I have to pause to remember how to spell, and which I am told can be pronounced two different ways, depending upon whether your Latin is Church or ancient. Well, mine is neither, and I will confess that when I first thought of a Latin title combining "principia" (as in principia ethica, mathematica, etc.) and the Latin for "writing," I was convinced the idea was somewhat humorous. The irony of such a ridiculously pretentious title, I felt, would be obvious to all. This has — to be blunt — not been so; in fact, this title has done much to confuse. Instead of the irony intended, the title itself has been found pretentious by some and simply unspeakable by others. In other words, better titles have been written.

A much better title, had it not been used before (this seems always to happen to me), would have been *Fathers and Sons*. In part, this is precisely what the play is about to me, as I look back on it; and at the time I wrote the play, this relationship between parent and child was certainly a preoccupation both in its obvious configurations — my relationship to my father, my child's relationship to me; and in the less obvious — myself as father interacting with myself as son.

The "fathers" then would be not only Bill's and Ernesto's literal fathers, those misunderstanding and misunderstood creatures referred to often in the first act, but also the literary fathers, the writers of Act II, along with the "mentors" discussed, and in one case even translated, by the "sons" in Act I — such as Ezra Pound and the author of *The Seafarer*. Again and again, as I read the play now, I find fathers who are there to give protection, comfort and courage to the "sons," and who invariably disappoint: be they the literary fathers of Act II, who though decent and well-meaning are unable to find any solutions in a world they now recognize as complicated and even solutionless; or the real fathers who maybe are not what they have seemed to their sons to be; or the Ezra Pounds who can be brilliant at one thing and despicable at another.

The "sons" too I now see everywhere, not only in Bill and Ernesto, but in the post-revolutionary country of Act II, itself young, enthusiastic, and the child of many fathers.

Reading *Principia Scriptoriae* again, trying to keep its writer always in mind as I have in preparation for writing this Introduction, I can't help but see everywhere in this play my fears of becoming a father and my frustrations at being a son—and all of this set in a location that is far, far away from any home.

During the writing of *Principia Scriptoriae*, one other incident occurred that affected some of the formulation of the play. In the summer of 1982, I was asked by Arena Stage in Washington to write a new adaptation of Dario Fo's farce *Accidental Death of an Anarchist*. I worked on this in 1983 and it opened to great success in January 1984. A New York producer, I was then told, had the rest of the U.S. rights to Fo's play and after seeing ours chose my version to be the one he would produce on Broadway. Fo's agent concurred, having seen our production twice. Fo himself had my script. The Broadway production opened in New York in late November, a few weeks *after* the presidential elections—not a terribly good time to open a political farce, what with everyone pretty much exhausted with political humor, intended or not. It received dreadful reviews and soon closed, though not before Fo himself disowned my adaptation and blamed it for the production's failure. This experience with a writer I greatly admired and had long looked up to shook me, and while writing *Principia Scriptoriae*, I struggled against letting it color my attitudes toward my play's "literary fathers." I hope I succeeded. In any event, the experience gave me much insight into where the worlds of art and power and ego clash and mesh, and forced me to focus on many of the questions concerning what a writer does, and what his place in society is—themes my play attempts to explore.

After reading in Seattle, the play had two full productions, the first at the Manhattan Theatre Club in New York and the second by the Royal Shakespeare Company in London. It was the latter, again directed by David Jones (in fact, this play was produced in England before *Between East and West*), in a wonderful production, which received the attention and understanding I had long hoped my writing would command.

I have never before tried to write about my work; rereading this introduction makes me no less leery about this activity than when I began. A play, of course, is only one small part autobiography, and so very much else. As I mentioned, many, many things go into the mix, making even what was once drawn from one's own life very distant, if not completely new. And I still question the value of discussing how I see my plays, as this effort smacks of self-involvement, which more that anything is anathema to playwriting, where one constantly must be aware of one's audience and the space between the playwright and it.

Whatever I say about my plays is only that — what I say and nothing more. What really counts is what the plays are themselves — so here they are, two plays that I hope complement each other in many interesting ways.

Richard Nelson
New York, May 1991

PRINCIPIA SCRIPTORIAE

For Tom Creamer
and Gerry Freund

Principia Scriptoriae was first performed on March 25, 1986 at The Manhattan Theatre Club (Lynne Meadow, Artistic Director), with the following cast:

BILL HOWELL	Anthony Heald
ERNESTO PICO	Joe Urla
MAN IN PRISON	Ernesto Gonzalez
JULIO MONTERO	Shawn Elliot
ALBERTO FAVA	George Morfogen
NORTON QUINN	Steven Gilborn
HANS EINHORN	Mike Nussbaum
SOLDIER	Ernesto Gonzalez
Director	Lynne Meadow
Set designer	John Lee Beatty
Costume designer	William Ivey Long
Lighting designer	Jennifer Tipton
Sound designer	Scott Lehrer
Production stage manager	Don Walters

Principia Scriptoriae was subsequently presented by The Royal Shakespeare Company in the Barbican Pit, London, on October 1, 1986 with the following cast:

BILL HOWELL	Anton Lesser
ERNESTO PICO	Sean Baker
MAN IN PRISON	Arturo Venegas
JULIO MONTERO	Clive Merrison
ALBERTO FAVA	Clive Russell
NORTON QUINN	Oliver Ford Davies
HANS EINHORN	David de Keyser
SOLDIER	Seven Elliott
Director	David Jones
Set designer	Bob Crowley
Costume designer	Fotini Dimou
Lighting designer	Paul Armstrong
Sound designer	Andrew Ludlam
Stage management	Tana Russell, Eric Lumsden, Susan Dale

THE CHARACTERS

BILL HOWELL
ERNEST PICO
MAN IN PRISON
JULIO MONTERO
ALBERTO FAVA
NORTON QUINN
HANS EINHORN
SOLDIER

NOTE

Each scene has a title that should be projected moments before the appropriate scene begins, remain in view throughout the scene, and go out when the scene ends (e.g., PRINCIPIUM 1: CHOOSE YOUR SETTING CAREFULLY).

THE SETTING

Latin America.

THE TIME

1970 and 1985.

SCENE ONE

Projection:
PRINCIPIUM I:
CHOOSE YOUR SETTING CAREFULLY

1970. Latin America. A poorly lit room without windows. Door barely visible upstage. A bench to one side. BILL HOWELL *and* ERNESTO PICO, *both in their early 20s, sit on rusted and bent lawn chairs, and talk.*

(Pause.)
BILL: Maybe a million. Depends on who is doing the counting. You understand that, don't you? That it does very much depend upon who is doing the counting.
ERNESTO: I understand.
BILL: So a million people. At least. All coming down Pennsylvania Avenue. What that must look like to Johnson. Think about that. You have to think about that. What Johnson must have thought. Or whoever it was they had holding down the fort, so to speak. *(Chuckles to himself.)* I'd have gotten my tail out of there fast if I was one of them. *(Short pause.)* Over a million people, Ernesto, think of that.
ERNESTO: Yeh. *(Short pause.)* That's something. That is really something.
BILL: The whole god damn government is crumbling. That's what it felt like while we were marching. Like the buildings themselves were toppling. I'm not joking. All the statues. The columns. The private Cabinet dining rooms. *(He laughs.)* The Senate handball courts.
(He laughs. Stops. Short pause. Then ERNESTO *laughs.)*
ERNESTO: Yeh. *(Short pause.)* So where were you? In the middle, I'll bet.

BILL: Yeh. *(Short pause.)* In the middle.
ERNESTO: Right! Hell.
(He slaps Bill on the leg. Pause.)
BILL: Ernesto, things are changing so fast and I do not mean little bitty changes either. I swear to you, in what, something like ten, give it fifteen years — it might only be five, who the hell really knows for sure — but the way things are done in the States is hardly going to be recognizable to us today. To people today. It is all going to be so — completely different. You'll have all these — different people running the place for one. That's one big thing. God can some of them talk, Ernesto. You should have heard them speak at the Mall. *(Short pause.)* You couldn't really hear them at the Mall. But God could they talk.
ERNESTO: I'll bet. *(Short pause.)* Of course they've got a lot to talk about.
BILL: The United States of America is going to be one very strange place in a few years. Given just a few more years, it is going to be one great place all right. All this is only the beginning. It is when you get people cooperating, sharing is really the word. We are sharing now. We are finally doing that. Some of us are. So once this has been firmly established, which it really is now, then we can finally quit all that "competition" stuff. I mean, what the hell are we competing for? We're all on the same planet, right? *(Short pause; he shakes his head.)* Not only do you have to think it, Ernesto, you must also live it. *(Pause.)* You understand that, right?
ERNESTO: I think so.
BILL: Good. *(Short pause.)* And this is precisely why I said — I mean, here I am a writer, right — but here I said, sure, I'll be the one to sell the T-shirts. Just tell me what the hell to do and I'll do it. *(Short pause.)* So I did.
ERNESTO: Huh.
(Short pause.)
BILL: Yeh. I sold the T-shirts. Someone had to. Ernesto, you have to keep remembering that there is nothing you are too good for. That is what sharing means. That is what it means today. *(Short pause.)* You talk revolution then you have to mean revolution and that goes for even revolting inside yourself. This is really the clue for the whole thing. You can't ever stop asking yourself questions. That is how you find out who

you are and also who you are not. It is not all just the outside world, it is the inside world of your brain too. But you know what I mean.

ERNESTO: Huh.

BILL: Ernesto, you get all of that into your head and the rest just falls into place.

(Pause.)

ERNESTO: When did you sell T-shirts?

BILL: When? In the march, Ernesto. The march on Washington. The Mall. What do you think I've been talking about?

ERNESTO: You sold T-shirts on the Mall?

BILL: Yeh.

ERNESTO: I thought you were in the middle of the march.

BILL: Yeh. In the middle selling T-shirts. *(Short pause.)* Ernesto, someone had to sell them. That's how we paid for the bus. I paid for the bus. *(Short pause.)* For part of it. That's how I was in the middle of things. I didn't just march, I also sold T-shirts. The actual march was a lot more than just marching. You can understand that, can't you? That a march is more than marching? That is everything I have been talking about.

ERNESTO: I understand, Bill.

BILL: I would think you would.

ERNESTO: I was confused for a second, but I understand now.

BILL: I was being very clear, I thought.

ERNESTO: Huh.

(Pause.)

BILL: If you've got a problem understanding, believe me, I can appreciate that. The one thing I do not want to do is come on too strong. Trust me about that, Ernesto. There is nothing wrong with not completely understanding. It has taken me years and years to figure that out. So just don't worry about it. *(Short pause.)* After all, I know you people have not exactly worked things out for yourselves yet. And that I can appreciate. That's not a problem for me. If anything, I am only amazed at how slow you all are at getting things going for yourselves. But that, I do not mean critically.

ERNESTO: Give us time, Bill.

BILL: I'd give you all the time in the world, if I could.

ERNESTO: Well time is all we need. We do after all have a different rhythm down here. From the States, I mean.

BILL: I appreciate that. *(Short pause.)* It wouldn't hurt though for you people to see the sort of thing I have been describing. I am only saying maybe you could find something in it to learn.

ERNESTO: Bill . . .

BILL: And that is not a criticism. Who still can't learn something? I can still learn something. That's all I'm saying. I'm talking about sharing, Ernesto; I am not being critical. *(Pause.)* Maybe it's just learning how to sell T-shirts.

(He looks at ERNESTO. They both laugh. Pause.)

BILL: How long do you think they'll make us wait in here?

(ERNESTO shrugs.)

ERNESTO: Can't be too long. My father's a lawyer.

BILL: A lawyer? Huh. *(Short pause.)* If I hadn't been a writer, I'd have been a lawyer. For unions.

ERNESTO: Good for you.

BILL: Must be fairly difficult being a lawyer in a country like this. The things you'd have to accept — people being picked up right off the streets and everybody just seems to accept —

ERNESTO: People are not accepting it, Bill.

BILL: That's not how it looks, Ernesto. Believe me.

ERNESTO: I can't help how it looks.

(Pause.)

BILL: I'll bet if it weren't for me being American, they'd be beating the shit out of us right now. That is what is standing in the way. Not your father being a lawyer.

ERNESTO: Bill, I don't think you know what you're . . .

BILL: Because I am an American, they can't. They wouldn't dare. I'm right, aren't I? It makes you sick. What a place to have to call home. *(Beat.)* Sorry. I know I've only been down here a week, but still, it must be very hard to call a place like this home.

ERNESTO: I don't.

BILL: Don't what?

ERNESTO: Call this place home.

BILL: Why not?

ERNESTO: Because, dammit Bill, I don't! That's why. *(Short pause.)* It may be my home, but I don't have to call it that. Why do you think I went to school in England? If anything made me not call this home, it's my going to school in England. You wouldn't believe how ignorant people are here. *(Pause.)*

BILL: People can be ignorant in England too, Ernesto. *(Short pause.)* At least they could when I was over there with a group from my college.

ERNESTO: I know that, but that's not what I'm saying. I am saying I don't call this home and people are unbelievably, relentlessly ignorant here. I am saying two different things. *(Short pause.)* And I came back—because of both things. I had to find out about me first. Then I came back. I know who I am now. I didn't before, now I do.

BILL: You know who you are now?

ERNESTO: I think so. Yes.

BILL: Terrific. It's great to know who you are. You're lucky.

ERNESTO: Yes. I think I am actually.

BILL: I'm still looking for myself. That's why I went away for a while, you know. Why I'm here in fact.

ERNESTO: I thought you came down to help us. You had read about us.

BILL: I did. Yes, I did. But I also came to look for myself. You can do them both, Ernesto. At least you can now. *(Short pause.)* First I thought I'd just go to Cuba. And that is where I'd be if I hadn't come down here. It turned out being a lot cheaper coming down here. *(Short pause.)* I came standby.

ERNESTO: You got standby from Kennedy?

BILL: It was no problem. You should remember that.

ERNESTO: Yeh. I should.

BILL: Still. I almost went to Cuba. I would have had to have gotten a flight from Paris. And it just didn't seem to be the time for Paris, you know what I mean? A couple of years ago, well sure; but I don't think there is much there now—for me at least; not after what I've been doing at home. Even Sartre's pretty much out of the picture these days. *(Short pause.)* He's going blind, you know.

ERNESTO: Yeh. Like Joyce. Like Borges. It's almost a trend.

BILL: I guess. Yeh. *(Short pause.)* Still it can't be at all like it must have been with Camus around. *(Short pause.)* Or—in the thirties. If I had been a self-exile in the thirties, they would have had to have tied me down to keep me away from Paris. *(Short pause.)* Or was it the twenties? *(Short pause.)* Anyway, you could not have kept me away from Paris. But today? Paris is going in the wrong direction today, Ernesto, if you want to know my opinion. Even Stockholm's got to be more interesting than Paris today, what with all the draft dodgers. I'm told the Swedes just roll out the red carpet for the draft dodgers—because it's not what they think of when they think of Americans, which basically means they don't have bombs and napalm coming out of their ears, which is how they should see some of us; how I would see some of us, that is except for the rest of us; anyway that's why I think the Swedes like them so much. Especially the black draft dodgers. Also there's all that free health care. *(Short pause.)* They know what they're doing in Sweden. Damn. *(Short pause.)* Well, I could have gone there, but it isn't cheap at all. Not like this. Anyway Paris is not where it's happening. And as for Cuba, I couldn't afford it in the end. It was that simple. Cuba is not cheap.

ERNESTO: You're not the first person to tell me that.

BILL: For some reason you would think it would be, right? But it's not. Sort of like San Franciso. Wouldn't you think San Francisco would be pretty damn cheap? Guess again. Of course, you can always live anywhere cheaply—if you're into that—but if not then it is a very expensive city as interesting American cities go. Denver, for one, is a lot cheaper. For some reason I'd have thought it would be the other way around—because of the mountains, I guess. But still, if you can afford San Francisco, it is worth every penny.

ERNESTO: It is?

BILL: Every centimo, believe me. And for writers like us, Christ, I mean you've got Berkeley, you've got City Lights Books . . .

ERNESTO: City Lights Books?

BILL: Don't tell me you don't know City Lights? Ernesto, you call yourself a writer and you don't know City Lights? Now they are really into poetry. And even more important they are into poets. They're into writing per se. They are incredible. They were thinking of publishing my novel; it turns out they can't of course, but they were really thinking about it. Said they'd put it in the window of the bookshop—they've got a bookshop, that's mostly what they are, a bookshop, and it has a very big window, so they'd put it in when I did get it published. I was really pleased with that.

ERNESTO: You should be. I would be.

BILL: I was floating, Ernesto.

ERNESTO: I'm not surprised.

BILL: You wouldn't believe the writers that go into that bookshop. There are writers all the time in that bookshop. It's intimidating, really.

ERNESTO: It would be. For me too. So it's San Francisco then, that's the place to go.

BILL: In my book it is, Ernesto.

ERNESTO: In your novel you mean? It's set in San Francisco?

BILL: No, that's just an expression. "In my book" means, well, it means—yes.

ERNESTO: Ah.

(Pause.)

BILL: My novel's set in St. Louis. That's not a place you want to go. *(Pause.)* I've been looking for a place to set my next book. Maybe down here. I'd say almost definitely down here, except it might be hard not knowing the language.

ERNESTO: You must know some Spanish though.

BILL: No. None. I know French *(Beat.)* I know some French.

ERNESTO: But the leaflets we were handing out when . . . Bill, they were in Spanish.

BILL: Yeh. So?

ERNESTO: You were handing out leaflets and you didn't know what they said?

BILL: I knew what they said. You don't have to know the language to know what they said—generally. *(Short pause.)* Oh come on. Did you read them?

ERNESTO: I wrote them.

BILL: Well there you have it. So what's the problem?

(Short pause.)

ERNESTO: But Bill . . .

BILL: *(Standing up)* What's the big fucking deal? *(Moving away)* I thought you wrote poetry. *(Pause.)* Look, we'll be out of here soon. I'm American, right?

(Pause. After a moment BILL goes upstage, unzips his pants, and pees against the wall.)

BILL: *(While peeing)* I did this once on the White House gate.

SCENE TWO

Projection:
PRINCIPIUM 2:
ALWAYS LIKE YOUR CHARACTERS

The same. BILL *and* ERNESTO *have metal plates full of food on their laps. Throughout the scene they eat. As the scene begins, they are chuckling.*

ERNESTO: Isn't that a character?
BILL: Still, every Englishman is a bit of a character.
ERNESTO: *(Giggling)* Even for an Englishman, Bill. *(He laughs. Pause.)* I love it when you come across people like that. This man would have forgotten to eat. He was that bad. Really. I swear to you, if it hadn't been for his wife, he'd have been — there would be nothing there. You could not make up such a character. *(Beat.)* If it hadn't been for his wife. *(Beat.)* If it hadn't been for her. *(Laughs.)* Sweet man, really. Brilliant. His book on Milton. Standard now, I think. *(Short pause.)* I wrote a poem about him. *(Beat.)* Part of it was about him. *(Short pause.)* And you've never been to Cambridge?
BILL: I told you, I've been to Oxford. *(Short pause; he takes a bite of food.)* I went punting there. Just outside Oxford.
ERNESTO: Just outside?
BILL: I went through Oxford to get just outside.
(Short pause.)
ERNESTO: Two different places, Cambridge and Oxford.
(They eat.)
BILL: So he never found out about you and his wife?
ERNESTO: *(Shakes his head.)* I told you his head was — *(Gestures "out there.")* He was quite a good tutor though. *(Pause.)* So was his wife. *(Laughs. Long pause.)* You know — it's not at all like everyone says it is. *(Beat.)*
BILL: *(Eating)* Prison?
ERNESTO: Cambridge, Bill. English universities in general, actually. *(Short pause.)* Oxbridge, I mean. *(Short pause.)* They're not all homosexual.

BILL: Who said they were?
ERNESTO: Everyone did — before I left. Everyone who talked to my mother did. You wouldn't believe the bizarre conversations my mother and I had before I left. It is not often that a son gets such a clear picture of just how his mother's mind works. There is a good reason for that. There is a humane reason for that. *(Short pause.)* Here is this nice upper-middle-class lady — and what does she start to do: take her only son around to brothels.
BILL: You're kidding.
ERNESTO: Mind you, the better brothels, but still.
BILL: That is pretty amazing.
ERNESTO: I'm not saying she went in. God forbid. She just took me around.
BILL: I'm glad she didn't go in.
ERNESTO: No. She stayed outside. She just hung around outside. And paid. *(Laughs.)* This is true. There can be some really strange shit down here. People can be really fucked up down here.
BILL: People can be fucked up anywhere. Take St. Louis.
ERNESTO: Uh-huh. *(Beat.)* She'd pay and stay outside. But first they'd have to haggle though. I'm standing there and they are haggling over the price. My mother and the prostitute. *(Short pause.)* That sort of does something to one's sense of pride. *(Short pause.)* And none of it would have happened if the priest hadn't told her about English universities. The ideas people get into their heads.
BILL: Right. Once they latch onto something, it doesn't matter what the truth is. How obvious the truth is.
ERNESTO: Especially when you're talking about a place they've never been. Like Cambridge. Or Oxford.
BILL: I know a lot of people like that. *(Beat.)* Almost everybody where I grew up is like that. *(Beat.)*
ERNESTO: That's not to say that some shit doesn't happen at English universities. Of course it does, but hell no one is pushing anyone around, they've still got English manners after all. Now there's something you don't find here.
BILL: No. You only find English manners in England, I'm afraid.
ERNESTO: Yeh. I think you're right. I am sure you are right. It's a shame too. Still, it turned out that there were prostitutes

even in Cambridge. So I wrote my mother that and she raised my allowance. *(He laughs. Pause.)*

BILL: I gave up taking an allowance when I went off to school. I thought that was part of the point of going off to school. *(Short pause.)* Of course I didn't go halfway around the world.

ERNESTO: Right.

BILL: And it doesn't take all that much to live in Ann Arbor. I had my dorm room. My meals. But I certainly didn't have money for prostitutes — even if I'd have wanted one. Which of course I didn't.

ERNESTO: Of course.

BILL: No offense.

ERNESTO: Please. From what I understand about American universities there is no need for prostitutes.

BILL: True. *(He smiles.)* This is very true. *(He laughs.* ERNESTO *laughs.)*

ERNESTO: I sometimes wish I had gone to an American university instead.

(They eat. Pause.)

BILL: And what about your father, Ernesto?

ERNESTO: About the brothels? He went by himself. He didn't go with my mother. I don't think he went with my mother.

BILL: I mean, what did he think of what your mother was doing?

ERNESTO: Why should he think anything? *(Beat.)* Maybe he didn't even know. I don't know. And what the hell, it was none of his business anyway, this was one of those special mother-son things, you know.

BILL: Huh. *(Short pause.)* Odd, isn't it?

ERNESTO: Not really. Not for here.

BILL: No, and that is what's odd — that we have such different backgrounds, Ernesto.

ERNESTO: That shouldn't surprise you.

BILL: Mine is so — I don't know — forgettable, I guess. At least that's what I figure I have to do — forget it — if I really want to be, become, what I know I want to become. But yours is so —

ERNESTO: Mine is so what?

BILL: Literary almost. You know what I mean.

ERNESTO: No, I don't think I do. How is my mother taking me to brothels literary? Seems to me that is the exact opposite of literary. That is what I would call not literary.

BILL: But Ernesto, come on, it sounds like it came right out of

a book—out of a Spanish novel say. Your mother taking you to brothels is so, it's picaresque really. Surely you see that.
ERNESTO: Picaresque?
BILL: Yeh.
ERNESTO: It's not picaresque, it's true. It happened.
BILL: Of course it happened. And that is just my point. Ernesto, no offense intended, but as a writer you seem to have it so god damn easy that's all.
BILL: I have what easy?
BILL: You seem to have stories—like this one with your mother and the brothels—that must just write themselves. That just need to be written down. And that's why I envy you.
ERNESTO: You envy me?
BILL: If you had come from St. Louis you'd know exactly what I was saying and why, believe me.
ERNESTO: But what about all that's happening now in the States? That seems to be a pretty good story to me.
BILL: It is. Of course it is. But for a journalist more than for someone like me. You understand the difference? What is happening in the States may be a little bit literary but basically it is journalistic. I think that is clear to everybody, Ernesto. So look, I'm not expecting you to agree, I just want you to understand what I am saying—that it seems to me that it has got to be a lot easier for you to write, that's all. That is all I want to say.
ERNESTO: That it is a lot easier for me to write?
BILL: Yes. *(Beat.)* Look, you've got a character like your mother and you're telling me it's not easier?
ERNESTO: She's my mother, she's not a character.
BILL: Don't tell me you haven't thought about writing about her.
ERNESTO: I don't want to write about my mother.
BILL: No?
ERNESTO: No.
(Pause.)
BILL: Then I'll write about her. Tell me some more about her.
ERNESTO: I don't want you writing about my mother. You never even met my mother.
BILL: I know she took you to brothels. That's a pretty good start, I can build off of that.
ERNESTO: Damn it, I told you she is not a character!!

BILL: I'll treat her sympathetically. I always try to like my characters.

ERNESTO: She is not your character!!! *(He moves away.)*

BILL: Sorry. *(Beat.)* Sorry.

ERNESTO: What are you doing down here anyway?

(Long pause.)

BILL: What were we talking about? Cambridge. Right. Cambridge.

(Short pause. ERNESTO *comes back, sits and continues to eat.)*

ERNESTO: It's not the homosexuals who are everywhere in Cambridge.

BILL: No?

ERNESTO: It's the politicians. The sons of the politicians. They send their sons from all over the world to be politicians. Shahs' sons. African tribal leaders' sons. *(Short pause.)* They do nothing. They know nothing. It's all just to say they went to Cambridge. No wonder they think of us the way they do. The Europeans, I mean. *(Beat.)* Can't blame them, really. *(Short pause.)* You know I couldn't even talk to the African Negro kids. No one could. Couldn't speak English. What the hell were they doing taking up space some smart English kid could have used? Couple of Indian kids I could talk to. That was it. The ones from down here — one of Somoza's kids was there — acted like they were retarded. The worst accents I have ever heard. Makes you embarrassed to say where you come from, really. *(Beat.)* Those accents like fingernails over a blackboard.

(Pause.)

BILL: And what about you?

ERNESTO: What about me?

BILL: How did you end up there?

ERNESTO: I earned the right to be there. *(Short pause.)* I earned the right. *(Pause.)* You would have thought I was English the way I fit in there. *(Short pause.)* I wasn't like the others who came there. I had a lot of English friends. You don't know what that means to people down here. You don't understand shit about us here — so just shut up.

BILL: Sorry.

ERNESTO: Don't apologize. *(Beat.)* Just shut up.

(Pause. They eat.)

ERNESTO: Fucking Americans. Don't even bother to learn the language. Don't know shit.

BILL: I heard that.

ERNESTO: Right.

(Pause.)

BILL: This food sucks. If I weren't so hungry, I wouldn't go near it.

ERNESTO: What did you expect—fried jumping beans?

(Short pause.)

BILL: No. I thought maybe Yorkshire pudding.

(They look at each other. Pause. They eat.)

BILL: Before I walk out of here, I'd love to have a good look around. Wonder who else they've got locked up. Could do a nice piece about this place. I'm not above writing journalism. There's a whole tradition of novelists writing journalism. *(Beat.)* People should know what is going on here. I mean, at home they should.

ERNESTO: Why?

(He eats. Pause.)

SCENE THREE

Projection:
PRINCIPIUM 3:
REMEMBER IT IS 99% PERSPIRATION

The same. An older man now sits on a bench to one side. He holds his head in his hands; he is barefoot.

(As lights come up, BILL is walking away from the man and toward ERNESTO, who sits in one of the chairs. Their clothes are now stained with sweat, their shirts unbuttoned.)

BILL: He doesn't speak English. You talk to him. *(He takes his handkerchief out and wipes his face and neck.)* You talk to him. *(Beat.)* Ask him who he is. *(*ERNESTO *doesn't move.)* Maybe he knows something. Maybe he knows why the fuck we're still in here. *(Beat.)* Shit, it's close in here. But I guess this kind of heat doesn't bother you people.

ERNESTO: It bothers us people.

(Pause.)

BILL: It is one thing to detain you for a while. They do this in the States, too. They're not supposed to but they got ways to do this too. But when they start throwing you in with other . . .

ERNESTO: *(Getting up)* Bill, give me your handkerchief.

BILL: What do you want with my . . . ? *(ERNESTO nods toward the man.)* It's filthy.

ERNESTO: You're using it.

BILL: It's my filth. *(BILL reluctantly hands him the handkerchief; ERNESTO goes to the man.)*

BILL: Ask him what he is in for. That's what I want to know. I've just heard that sometimes they put murderers in with people like us — just to scare us.

ERNESTO: Where did you hear that?

BILL: I heard it. I heard it.

ERNESTO: *(To man, handing him the handkerchief)* Tome esto. Haber si le ayuda. [Here. This will help.]

MAN: Si. Gracias. [Yes. Thank you.]

ERNESTO: ¿Sabé usted, le dijeron porque . . . ? [Did they tell you why . . .]

MAN: No, no se nada. No me dijeron nada. Estaba caminando mi perro cuando me . . . [No. I don't know anything. They told me nothing. I was walking my dog when they . . .] *(He turns away, holding his head. Pause. ERNESTO returns to BILL.)*

BILL: Well?

ERNESTO: He was just out walking his dog.

BILL: He was arrested for walking his dog? Right. Right.

ERNESTO: I didn't say that. I don't think he meant that.

BILL: You think just because we give him a handkerchief he's not going to try and pull something. Don't be so naive, Ernesto. *(ERNESTO looks at him.)* How fucking naive. I don't know how you survived this long in the world, Ernesto. *(Laughs.)*

ERNESTO: I gave him the handkerchief, Bill, because he was bleeding.

BILL: I know that. *(Short pause.)* But I'm talking about in the bigger sense — you also gave him the handkerchief so he wouldn't do anything to us. I know he was bleeding. *(Laughs to himself again.)* People aren't the way you like them to be, Ernesto. If he's going to do something, he is going to do something. Handkerchief or no handkerchief. Period. You can't change that.

ERNESTO: Why are you so sure he's dangerous?

BILL: He's in jail, isn't he?

ERNESTO: We're in jail, are we dangerous?

(Pause.)

BILL: Ernesto, when we were handing out the leaflets and that man came up to you. He said what again?

ERNESTO: I told you.

(ERNESTO gets up, BILL follows him.)

BILL: Tell me again. Maybe we missed something.

ERNESTO: What's there to miss, he said to be sure to pick up any leaflets that might be dropped.

BILL: Which we did. Dammit, we did that!

ERNESTO: Bill . . .

BILL: We fucking did that!

ERNESTO: Bill, they didn't put us in here just for littering.

BILL: I know that. *(Beat.)* Of course I know that. What do you think I am? I was just thinking out loud. Can't I think out loud?

ERNESTO: Think out loud.

(Pause.)

BILL: You think I'm panicking, don't you? I'm not, Ernesto. I am nowhere near to panicking.

ERNESTO: Good.

BILL: You don't believe me, do you? Come on. How can I convince you? Tell me how I can convince you.

ERNESTO: Look, you already have.

BILL: I have?

ERNESTO: Yes, Bill.

BILL: Good. *(Short pause.)* How did I convince you?

ERNESTO: Bill!!!

BILL: All I'm asking is . . .

MAN: ¿Qué tiempo hace que están aquí? [How long have you been here?]

(BILL and ERNESTO stop. Short pause.)

MAN: ¿Hace cuanto tiempo que están aqui?

ERNESTO: Horas. Como cinco. Bueno, ahora no estamos seguros. [Hours. Maybe five. We're not really sure anymore.]

BILL: *(In a half-whisper)* What did he say? *(Beat.)* What did he say, Ernesto?

ERNESTO: *(Ignoring BILL, going to the man)* ¿Y usted? [And you?]

MAN: ¿Semanas? ¿Qué mes es éste? [Weeks? What month is it?]

ERNESTO: Marzo. [March.]

MAN: Meses entonces. [Months then.]

BILL: Ernesto!

MAN: ¿Les entendí bien que ustedes estaban distribuyendo panfletos? [Did I understand right that you were passing out leaflets?]

ERNESTO: *(Nods. Then:)* ¿Entiende ingles, entonces? [Then you understand English?]

MAN: Algo. Un poco. ¿Panfletos izquierdistas? [Some. A little. Leftist leaflets?]

ERNESTO: El Frente Unido. Estaba yo en Inglaterra, sabe usted. Aun asi, realmente no esperaba . . . [The United Front. I've been in England. Still I didn't really expect . . .]

MAN: ¿Usted esperaba Speakers' Corner? [You expected Speakers' Corner?]

(ERNESTO laughs.)

BILL: What's funny? What is so god damn funny?

ERNESTO: I told him I'd been in England, so I wasn't prepared for this and he said what had I expected, Speakers' Corner.

(ERNESTO laughs again. BILL doesn't.)

BILL: Oh.

ERNESTO: No habiamos estado en la calle tanto tiempo, no, como menos de una hora. A lo maximo una hora. Ademas, no fueron panfletos radicales exactamente. Seguro que conoce usted la clase de material. [We hadn't been on the street that long. Less than an hour. At most an hour. They weren't exactly radical leaflets. I'm sure you know the kind of stuff.]

MAN: Yo vengo escribiendo esa clase de material por años. [I've been writing that kind of stuff for years.]

ERNESTO: ¿No me diga? ¿Es escritor? [Really? You're a writer?]

BILL: What? What? What did he say that's so interesting?

MAN: Yo escribo para *El Mundo*. ¿Ya les ha hablado alguien? [I write for El Mundo. Has anyone talked to you yet?]

ERNESTO: No. No.

BILL: Did he say *El Mundo*? Isn't that a newspaper?

MAN: Ya veo. [I see.]

BILL: Ernesto, that's a newspaper, right?

ERNESTO: A lo mejor conoce usted a mi padre. El ha escrito un poco para los periódicos también. Ferdinand Pico. [Maybe you know my father, he's done some journalism as well. Ferdinand Pico.] *(MAN nods)* ¿Le conoce? [You know him?] *(MAN nods.)*
BILL: What does he have to do with *El Mundo*?
ERNESTO: He's a journalist. He knows my father.
MAN: Prefiero hablar de otra cosa. [I'd rather talk about something else.]
ERNESTO: ¿Por qué no quiere hablar de mi padre? [Why don't you want to talk about my Father?] *(To BILL)* He doesn't want to talk about my father.
BILL: So he's a journalist. Big fucking deal. *(Goes to pull ERNESTO's arm.)* Come on. You've talked to him enough.
ERNESTO: Why won't he talk about my father?
(MAN stands and moves away.)
BILL: *(Pulling on ERNESTO)* Look, the cop, you sure you understood the cop, Ernesto.
ERNESTO: What cop?
BILL: The cop who picked us up for Christ sake.
ERNESTO: I don't know if he was a cop, Bill.
MAN: ¿El cree que el hombre que les arrestó era uno de los puercos de la policía? [He thinks the man who picked you up had to be a cop?] *(He laughs.)*
BILL: What did he say? *(To the man)* Shut up. *(To ERNESTO)* You told me he was a cop.
ERNESTO: I never did, Bill. I said he acted like a cop. Maybe he was one, maybe he wasn't.
BILL: Oh. *(Beat.)* Oh. They can't do any shit to us. *(Short pause.)* I won't take any shit. You said he knows your father. Ask him where the hell your father is.
ERNESTO: ¿Qué sabe usted de mi padre? [What do you know about my father?]
(The man spits. Ernesto is taken aback.)
BILL: What can they do, Ernesto? It's not like they found drugs on us or something. This is one country I wouldn't like to be in when they found drugs on me.
MAN: Ellos pueden decir que les encontraron drogas encima. [They can say they found drugs on you.]
(BILL turns to the man.)
ERNESTO: He says — they can say they found drugs on us.

BILL: But I didn't have any drugs. I don't travel with drugs.
MAN: ¿Y qué? [So?]
BILL: So they can't prove I did. He knows English?
ERNESTO: A little he said.
BILL: Oh. *(Beat.)* You were with me.
MAN: ¿El? ¿Quién le prestaría atención a éste? [Him? Who would listen to him?]
ERNESTO: *(Translating)* Me? Who would listen to me?
MAN: Quizás sea un asesino. Quizás un abusador de niños. [Maybe he's a murderer. Maybe a child molester.]
ERNESTO: Maybe I'm a murderer. Maybe I'm a child molester.
MAN: ¿Quién sabe lo que ha hecho? [Who knows what he's done?]
ERNESTO: Who knows what I've done?
MAN: ¿Después de todo, está en la prisión, no? [After all, he's in prison, isn't he?]
ERNESTO: After all, I'm in prison, aren't I?
(Short pause.)
BILL: Right. *(Beat.)* Right.

SCENE FOUR

Projection:
PRINCIPIUM 4:
WRITE OUT OF EXPERIENCE

The same. ERNESTO *and* BILL *on the floor, trying to sleep.*

(Pause.)
(From off we hear a round of automatic gunfire.)
(Pause.)
BILL: He'll be back. They'll bring him back. He's a journalist, right? *(Beat.)* He said he was a journalist, right? They're not about to . . . *(Beat.)* . . . to a journalist, Ernesto.
(Pause.)

ERNESTO: They fake shooting you. To frighten you. I read that somewhere.

BILL: Right. So that's what they're doing. I get it. *(Pause.)* I cannot believe this is happening to me. I can't believe I am experiencing this.

(BILL *gets up and goes to a small faucet in the wall, with a bucket under it. He turns the faucet on and sticks his head under the water.* ERNESTO *watches, then stands up.*)

ERNESTO: Good idea.

BILL: Sticky in here. I think it's night out, don't you?

ERNESTO: Yes. I do. *(He puts his head under the faucet.)* It feels like night. *(Beat.)* I can't sleep. Can't you?

BILL: *(Lying down again.)* It takes me awhile. Even — in college, it would usually take me awhile.

(ERNESTO *sits in one of the lawn chairs. Pause.*)

ERNESTO: *(Pointing to the other chair.)* Bill, mind if I . . . ?

BILL: What? *(Looks up at* ERNESTO *pointing.)* Mind if you what?

ERNESTO: The chair.

BILL: *(Turning over)* What are you asking me for?

ERNESTO: It's your chair.

BILL: Do whatever you want.

(ERNESTO *takes the other chair, sets it in front of him and uses it as a footrest.*)

BILL: *(Quietly)* It's not my chair.

(Pause.)

ERNESTO: My father does some journalism too. I don't mean "too" like — *(Points to the door.)* I wasn't talking about him. I mean — as well as being a lawyer. He does both. Though he tries to keep those two careers separate. When he can. *(Short pause.)* When he can. You'll meet him.

BILL: Yeh. I guess I will.

(ERNESTO *rubs his face. Pause.* BILL *rolls over and watches* ERNESTO.)

BILL: What that guy said about your father, it hasn't — you're not upset, are you?

ERNESTO: No, of course not.

BILL: Good. *(Rolls over.)*

ERNESTO: If it weren't for my father — I'd have never been a writer. You didn't know that, did you? You couldn't know that. *(Pause.)* Bill . . . ?

BILL: *(Still turned away)* I'm listening.

ERNESTO: You know it really takes that kind of immediate

encouragement—like I got from my father—to do anything here, something different here. It is almost impossible to fight your own family's wishes here. Oh you can try. My father tried. But it is hard here, Bill.

BILL: *(Turns, sits up.)* Ernesto . . .

ERNESTO: He didn't upset me!! *(Stands and walks to one side.)* My father would never have anything to do with the government. I know this. He has told me this. He wants nothing to do with it. He says—because he doesn't want to end up retiring to Miami. *(He laughs.* BILL *smiles.)* My grandmother wanted him to go into the government. She said, that's where the money is made. I don't think she's ever forgiven him, really. She still pressures him I think. *(He lifts his shirt and dries his face. Pause. He uses his shirt to fan his face.)* He wanted to go to Europe to university. His family had the money. We know they had the money. It wasn't the money. It cost a lot and they weren't rich but they could have gotten up the money. That's what Father always said. So he didn't go to Europe. Not for twenty years. *(Beat.)* Twenty years later I meet him at Heathrow. I think that's why he sent me to school in England, so I could meet him at Heathrow. *(Beat.)* In fact, from the time I was . . . there was never even a question. I was going. Not from anyone. Not from my sisters. *(Beat.)* My father screamed with joy when he saw me at Heathrow. *(Beat. He is fighting back tears.)* We fed the ducks. I knew he'd want to do something like that. Something English like that. *(Trying to laugh.)* When he first got off the plane, he looked to me like a bus conductor. But he was my father. *(Beat.)* A good man. Who'd have shit to do with the government. Shit! *(Beat.)* That's how he raised me. *(Pause.)*

BILL: Obviously the guy just didn't know what he was talking about.

ERNESTO: Obviously.

(Long pause.)

BILL: Look, even if he did meet . . .

ERNESTO: He didn't!!!!! *(Stands and moves to one side.)* He couldn't.

BILL: Right. I know that. *(Beat. Quietly.)* But even if he did, what is so wrong about being seen meeting Manuel Rosa? Rosa's a pretty well-known poet after all.

ERNESTO: He's the government's ambassador to Franco. *(Beat.)* My father would know what anyone would think if they saw

him meeting with Rosa. Poet or not, he's this government's ambassador to Spain. It's clear to anyone what meeting with him means.
(Pause.)
BILL: Then, the guy's wrong. It's that simple.
(Slowly ERNESTO *goes back and sits in the chair.)*
(Pause.)
ERNESTO: Read much of Rosa?
BILL: Maybe a couple of things in an anthology.
ERNESTO: He doesn't translate well. If you knew his love poems especially, there's little else like them in Spanish. *(Short pause.)* Incredible how you'd never guess Rosa's thinking from his poetry. He doesn't put any of that right-wing shit into his poetry. *(Short pause.)* You're right, Bill — the guy's simply wrong about my father. *(Long pause.)* Tell me about yours. Your father.
BILL: Ernesto . . .
ERNESTO: Please. I'd like to know.
BILL: *(Sits up again.)* He — teaches chemistry in a college. I grew up on a college campus. He doesn't read much. At least he doesn't read what I read. He reads a lot of journals. *(Pause.)* They must be very upset. My parents. My father becomes pathetic when there is nothing he can do. There is nothing he can do.
(Suddenly another round of automatic fire. Pause. ERNESTO *begins to sob.* BILL *gets up and pats him on the shoulder.* ERNESTO *hugs him. They hug. Finally* BILL *pulls away.)*
BILL: Hey, watch that hugging stuff. Remember, I know what kind of school you went to.
*(*ERNESTO *smiles.* BILL *smiles.)*

SCENE FIVE

Projection:
PRINCIPIUM 5:
LET YOUR IMAGINATION GO

The same. ERNESTO *sits in one of the chairs.* BILL *stands behind him.*

ERNESTO: A trial?
BILL: It's the only thing that makes sense. It's why they're keeping us. What other reason, Ernesto, could they have for keeping us? This happens in the States too.
ERNESTO: I don't know.
BILL: I'm sure of it. I'd bet on it. They're going to have to let us talk to your father.
ERNESTO: Leave my father out of this.
(Pause. ERNESTO *stands and moves away.* BILL *looks at him, then shrugs.)*
BILL: What the hell, we'll get Kunstler then. *(Laughs.)*
ERNESTO: Get who?
BILL: Never mind. The most important thing to keep in mind is how are we going to turn this into—like one of those happenings. That should be the idea. You know what I'm talking about right? *(Beat.)* Oh come on, you know about those. They had them in Greenwich Village, about ten years ago.
ERNESTO: Oh. *(Beat.)* Oh, right.
BILL: People like Cage and Rauschenberg. A lot of people like that. A lot of people who are somebody today, Ernesto. It's really amazing when you think of it.
ERNESTO: Amazing how many became somebody?
BILL: Yeh.
ERNESTO: I guess they must have found something together, something they could use later—as individuals.
BILL: I'm sure.
ERNESTO: That's what I've wanted, you know. To find such a group—of individuals. It's what I think I need, really.
BILL: Who doesn't? Who wouldn't like that? And who says it

can't happen here? This could be the start of that sort of thing, actually. Except with a big difference; with this we have to get political, those happenings, they really weren't. They happened too early to get political. But in style they can be the same.

ERNESTO: I understand.

BILL: There's also the stuff from the Chicago trial to learn from. Actually, historically, I do think that was when the happening moved into the political, moved ahead, so to speak, beyond just "art," you know with . . . *(Makes the gesture of quotation marks.)* and into the realm of politics, politics without . . . *(Makes the gesture of quotation marks.)* You know what I mean. Historically, Chicago is the turning point. Actually all this only proves what a teacher of mine was saying that in fact they are one and the same thing — art and politics, that is. As one develops into one, the other develops into the other. *(Beat.)* Something like that. I only took one semester from him. Anyway, each one has the other inside itself, that much I do remember.

ERNESTO: What Chicago trial?

BILL: The Chicago trial. With the pictures, you know, of the black guy gagged. The judge gagged the black guy. Which reminds me, one thing we have to hope to get, we have to do anything to get, is pictures.

ERNESTO: Pictures of what?

BILL: I am starting to see all the possibilities, Ernesto. As long as we keep Chicago in mind, we will be doing just fine. Look, if they want to ask us their fascist questions, hell, let them, who says we have to answer? Who says we can't say any damn thing we want to?

ERNESTO: I'm lost, Bill.

BILL: Just keep listening and it will all start coming together for you, I promise. Just listen. We are going to turn the whole god damn courtroom into the zoo it really is, Ernesto. It's going to be real theater, that's what it has to be — and that's where the happening stuff comes in. Understand now? *(Beat.)* Look. They won't know what to do, right? They never do. They didn't in Chicago. Hence — the black guy gets gagged. One of us could get gagged, Ernesto, that would be a trip. Let's not throw out any real possibility here. If they are like — and I'm sure they are — like they are everywhere else in the world, then the judge, we can make him look like a complete fool, Ernesto. This will be our job. *(Laughs to himself.)* We just have to keep interrupting him with: Oink! Oink! Oink!

ERNESTO: Oink?

BILL: Yeh. Oink. You know for . . .

ERNESTO: I know. I know.

BILL: So maybe we will be gagged. Maybe I will be. I don't know Spanish anyway so what's to lose, right? Now in Chicago, they also had people like Ginsberg. They were there from the beginning. Like camp followers. That really helped matters. They talked to the media and things. It's got to be a zoo outside of the trial too. Anyone like him down here?

ERNESTO: Ginsberg?

BILL: Yeh.

ERNESTO: Any poet here like Ginsberg?

BILL: He doesn't have to be a poet. But yeh. Like him. *(Beat.)* Sort of like him. Anything like him.

ERNESTO: No. *(Beat.)* No.

BILL: Oh, Well, somebody right will come along. There's always somebody. Maybe even a somebody we don't even know. Something like this is enough to make somebody's name. Whatever, all we have to do is keep—*(Begins to pound the chair on the floor.)* Oink! Oink! Fascists! Pigs! Oink! Oi . . .
(From the hall, we hear someone screaming as he is being brought by. The screaming gets louder as it passes the door, then fades in the distance. Pause.)

ERNESTO: Come on—oink! Oink! Oink!

BILL AND ERNESTO: Oink! Oink! Oink!

(As they yell, they begin to laugh.)

SCENE SIX

Projection:
PRINCIPIUM 6:
KNOW YOUR READER

The same. The light in the room is off though light now floods through the open door. The scene then is basically in silhouette.

   (ERNESTO *sits on the floor, against the wall. He holds his arm.* BILL *sits on the bench, his pants down. He rubs his thigh. Their clothes ripped, their faces bruised. In the silence we are able to hear, from down the hallway, a radio playing Spanish love songs sung by a woman.* BILL *coughs; blood comes up out of his mouth, in almost a chunk. He begins to wipe it away.*)
BILL: *(In obvious pain)* There's so much to write about, isn't there? *(Beat.)* Think about that. And that in and of itself is enough to keep you going. *(Pause.)* A minute ago I was thinking about Spenser. God knows why. I haven't thought about Spenser in —a very long time. I think I really would like to reread *The Faerie Queene*. I'd like to read it once when there wasn't a reason to read it. I mean, now that I'm not in school. It is an odd thing I'll bet to read when you are not in school. How's the shoulder?
ERNESTO: I'm sure they didn't set it right. I told them that. I can feel that they didn't set it right. *(Short pause.)* The bone is pressing through. I don't think the bones are even touching.
   (Pause.)
BILL: Fuck them.
   (ERNESTO *stands and goes to* BILL)
ERNESTO: Get on your back. Let me see.
   (BILL *does.* ERNESTO *looks him over.*)
ERNESTO: Shit. Stay there. *(He goes to the faucet, turns on the water, wets a part of his shirt which he has taken off. As he is filling the bucket:)* If you are looking for something to read . . .
BILL: Who said I was looking for something to read? I've got a million things to read. *(Beat.)* What do you suggest I should read?

ERNESTO: Lorca. *(He begins to rub the cloth over* BILL, *cleaning his wounds.)* There's a feeling Lorca has—in his love poems. I'm talking basically about his love poems. They are things unto themselves. About nothing—but themselves.

BILL: Huh? Are they sort of like Manuel Rosa's? *(*ERNESTO *stops rubbing and looks at him.)* Like you said about Manuel Rosa's love poems?

ERNESTO: No. *(He begins to rub again.)* They are nothing like his. Does this burn?

BILL: Yes.

ERNESTO: And this?

BILL: Yes.

(Beat.)

ERNESTO: What Lorca has, what I wouldn't give to get that into my poems.

BILL: How is he in translation?

ERNESTO: I don't know. I don't know. *(Beat.)* I'm thinking of taking your advice and writing about my family.

BILL: Don't listen to me.

ERNESTO: It'll end up being about me, of course. When I really write it.

BILL: That's happened to me too.

ERNESTO: There's school. *(Beat.)* There's growing up. *(Beat.)* There's my first sex.

BILL: With the prostitute?

ERNESTO: Who said my first sex was with the prostitute? *(Beat.)* Right. With the pros . . .

*(*BILL *suddenly coughs up more blood.* ERNESTO *looks at him, then turns away, fighting back tears.* BILL *begins to clean himself off.)*

BILL: *(While cleaning the blood)*
"Whan that Aprill with his shoures soote
The droghte of March hath perced to the roote,
And bathed every veyne in swich licour . . ."

ERNESTO: *(Without looking at* BILL*)*
"Of which vertu engendred is the flour."
(Pause.) So you know Old English too.

BILL: Middle English.

ERNESTO: Right. That's what I meant. Middle English. *(He takes the rag from* BILL *and begins to wipe the back of Bill's neck.)*

BILL: *The Seafarer's* Old English. *(Beat.)* I also took Old English. Middle English and Old English.
ERNESTO: Really? I never quite went that far. Greek. *(Pause.)* A little Greek.
(Pause.)
BILL: I even translated from the Old English.
ERNESTO: Like Pound.
BILL: Right. *(Beat.)* I was really into Pound then. *(Beat.)* Hard man to figure out, Pound.
ERNESTO: *(Going to the faucet to rinse out the rag)* How he could let the Fascists use him, you mean?
BILL: Yeh. *(Beat.)* Doesn't make any sense to me. From the poetry. *(Beat.)* From the great poetry.
ERNESTO: I know. *(Comes back and continues to clean BILL.)* Take out the anti-Semitism and it's really great poetry. How hard is it to breathe?
BILL: *(He breathes and shrugs.)* Not hard.
ERNESTO: Does this hurt?
BILL: No. (ERNESTO *nods and sighs.)* What does that mean? That it doesn't hurt?
ERNESTO: I don't know. *(Beat. They both laugh, though with pain.)* Old English? (BILL *nods.)* Wow.
(BILL *reaches and takes out his wallet and takes a piece of paper out.)*
ERNESTO: Let me.
BILL: I can do it. Sit down.
ERNESTO: What's that?
BILL: *(Takes the rag from* ERNESTO *and begins to wipe the blood off himself. He reads:)*
"So on myself I may utter fragments
of song, rehearse bits of my history,
how in labored days, hard ships hours
I so often suffered, the bitter heart's sorrow
had long lived through . . . "
ERNESTO: Yours?
BILL: My translation.
ERNESTO: That's what I meant. There've been so many translations.
BILL: When you take Old English you find there's not much there to translate but *The Seafarer.*
ERNESTO: I never thought about that. See, with Greek—
BILL: Greek's a whole different story.

ERNESTO: With Greek you could spend your whole life translating from the Greek.
BILL: People have.
ERNESTO: I suppose so.
BILL: I could think of worse ways of spending your life.
ERNESTO: Me too. *(Beat.)* Me too.
(Pause.)
BILL: I keep a copy in my wallet. They never took my wallet. Throughout all that they never took it.
ERNESTO: They took mine. First thing.
BILL: Soon they'll take mine.
ERNESTO: Yeh.
BILL: Next time they call us in. They'll take it then.
(ERNESTO has sat on the bench, and looks over BILL's shoulder.)
BILL: Can you read it in this light? *(ERNESTO nods. Reading:)*
" . . . how upon ships
I so ventured to homes of sorrow;
the terrible rollings of waves there kept me,
a close night-watch at ship's prow
which neared close against cliffs.
(Beat.)
I heard nothing but the sea's chord,
cold waves. Once the song of the whooper swan
gamed for me. The gannet's hoarse cry
and curlew's caw replaced a man's laugh,
seagull sang in place of mead."
BILL AND ERNESTO:
"Storms beat the staid-cliffs; the tern
shrieks back through iced feathers;
very often the eagle screams about;
no kinsman can comfort a desolate man."
(Long pause.)
ERNESTO: Wow. *(Beat.)* "No kinsman can comfort a desolate man." Sort of jumps out at you at the end. Sort of shocks you. It's beautiful. *(Short pause.)* What's a gannet?
BILL: *(Putting the paper back)* Some kind of bird. I forget what kind. *(Beat.)* I've never seen one. *(Beat.)* I had to look it up in the encyclopedia. *(Short pause.)* I've seen a whooper swan though. *(Taps his wallet.)* Next time, they'll take it. *(Puts it in his pocket. Pause.)* I passed out. *(Short pause.)* Did you pass out? *(ERNESTO doesn't move.)* I wanted to pass out. *(Pause.)* When they did that

to my cock, that's when I wanted to pass out. I passed out later. After they did this to my cock. *(Beat.)* Fuck them.
(ERNESTO starts to cry. BILL immediately stands up and now tries to keep ERNESTO from thinking about what has happened.)

BILL: Ernesto, do you ever have days when all you want to do is sit surrounded by your books?

ERNESTO: Bill . . .

BILL: To have all of my books around me, to be hugging them almost, to be hugging them really, I have days when that's all I want in the world. I've never told anyone this before. *(Beat.)* I have some beautiful old books. I think I've been to every used book store in the Midwest. *(Beat.)* The Upper Midwest. *(Beat.)* It's something I do.

ERNESTO: *(Sobbing now)* Bill . . .

BILL: *(Loud so as not to hear ERNESTO's crying)* Ernesto, that gannet's got me thinking. If one could just describe what a bird say, does — think of that — the way it flies. In words. Who wouldn't be pleased with doing that? Having accomplished something like that. *(Turns to ERNESTO.)* Am I right? *(ERNESTO nods.)* What do you think, maybe I'll write something about a gannet. What do you think one looks like? *(ERNESTO smiles and nods; he stands and goes to BILL.)*

BILL: And what are you going to write about? *(He is trying to keep from crying now.)* What are you going to write about?!! *(Pause.)*

ERNESTO: Cry if you want. I don't care if you cry.

BILL: *(Screams.)* What are you going to write about?!!!!!

ERNESTO: I don't know. My family. Me. I'll write about growing up.

BILL: What?

ERNESTO: *(Louder.)* I said I'll write about growing up.

BILL: Good. *(Beat.)* Good. *(Pause.)* Who doesn't like reading about somebody growing up?
(Pause. Intermission.)

SCENE SEVEN

Projection:
PRINCIPIUM 7:
IT SHOULD ALSO BE ENTERTAINING

A men's bathroom. Stall to one side. Fan overhead. The same Latin American country, 15 years later.

(JULIO MONTERO, *mid-40s and well-dressed, stands at the sink, looking into the mirror.* ALBERTO FAVA, *also well-dressed, sits on a stool to one side. He is a middle-aged Italian.* ERNESTO *leans against the door. They are all smoking.*)
(Pause.)

JULIO: *(Without looking at* ALBERTO*)* Did you see those pictures of his baby? *(Beat.)* Looks like a pig. His son looks like a pig. *(Beat.)* The son looks like the father.

ALBERTO: He looks like a baby.

JULIO: Not like babies we have here. Made me sick looking at that kid. *(Beat.)* Same feeling I get looking across the table at him. *(Beat.)* Hans Einhorn has hurt me, Alberto.

ALBERTO: So you keep saying.
(Short pause.)

JULIO: I am deeply hurt. I had not anticipated this fact that I was to be hurt, Alberto.

ALBERTO: Enthusiasm, Julio. Nothing is meant by honest enthusiasm. *(Beat.)* If you had let us sleep first. We haven't slept. We should not have met formally until tomorrow. I did suggest that. *(Beat.)* I am suggesting it again.

JULIO: No.

ALBERTO: *(Putting out his cigarette)* Hans did say you'd want us tired out.

JULIO: See what I'm saying? He doesn't stop. God damn Nazi. And you repeat it.
(Short pause.)

ALBERTO: Hans may be many things, Julio, but a Nazi he is not. You've read him.

JULIO: I haven't read him. *(Beat.)* I know what Einhorn writes without having to read him.
ALBERTO: You two were just talking about his last novel.
JULIO: I can talk about things I have not read. *(Beat.)* I'm human. *(Short pause.)* Where does he get this holier-than-thou attitude? In the end, it's this which gets under the skin. And don't say it is honest enthusiasm. This is how this man thinks. It has not been easy to sit and take what he has been saying.
ALBERTO: Such as? *(Beat.)* For example?
JULIO: I have no examples. I have my feelings. Hans Einhorn has greatly upset me. You don't upset me. The American writer doesn't upset me. Even though he is a Republican he doesn't upset me.
ALBERTO: I hardly imagine that Quinn is a Republican.
JULIO: He is, Alberto. He may not even know it himself, but he is. *(Beat.)* Watch him. I've been watching him. You watch him.
(Beat.)
ALBERTO: Watch him do what?
JULIO: Act like an American Republican. *(Pause.)* You're not going to ask me how an American Republican acts? *(Pause.)* They act in funny ways, especially when they are negotiating, which they are doing right now with our people. Very funny ways, Alberto. You mention say—socialist economic policy; or—revolutionary freedom force, or—
ALBERTO: Julio . . .
JULIO: . . . and they begin to stare at the ends of their pens, they stare and twirl their pens. They are biding their time, you see, thinking all this is just bullshit we have to get flushed out . . .
ALBERTO: Shut up!
(Pause.)
JULIO: Those are the Republicans. *(Beat.)* But I like Quinn. He's not the one who upsets me.
ALBERTO: How long are you going to stay in the bathroom?
JULIO: It is my fucking bathroom. *(Beat.)* It is the People's fucking bathroom.
(They smile at each other; JULIO *turns back to the mirror.)*
JULIO: Look at the gray, Alberto. Soon I shall look as old as you. *(He glances at* ALBERTO *and smiles.* ALBERTO *just looks at him.)* And dye my hair too. You do dye your hair, don't you, Alberto?

ALBERTO: Are we going back into the meeting?

JULIO: Tell me something, Alberto . . .

ALBERTO: I don't dye my hair!

JULIO: Not that. Not that. *(Beat.)* Are you sure? *(Beat.)* I wasn't going to ask that. Tell me, why you, Alberto? Why a man like you? I have so much admired you. And not just the writing—yours I have read, Alberto—but what you have done. Where you have placed your influence. As one leftist to—*(Gestures to* ALBERTO, *then turns away and looks back into the mirror.)* And I find you now involved with this right-wing American group.

ALBERTO: I would not call The Writers Committee for Human Rights a right-wing organization, Julio.

JULIO: No? *(Laughs.)*

ALBERTO: And its offices are in London, not America.

JULIO: London, New York, you are splitting hairs now, Alberto. *(Laughs, looks back into the mirror.)* Five hours' sleep. That is all one needs. Too much sleep and you get wrinkles. Did you know that?

ALBERTO: Julio, if we are so god damn right wing, why are we here? Why are we wasting our time?

JULIO: I don't know. I don't know.

ALBERTO: You asked us, Julio! You invited us!!

JULIO: Not to argue. *(Beat.)* Not to be hurt. I invited what I thought was a few friends—fellow writers—to see my country. To show it off; there are many interesting aspects of my country to write about. The literacy rate, for instance, in the last three years . . .

ALBERTO: We received the literature—at our hotel. Thank you.

JULIO: This Writers Committee for Human Rights has been slandering us. We needed to do something.

ALBERTO: So do it! That's all we're asking for. *(Beat.)* Then sit down and explain why you can't. If there's a rational explanation for keeping Manuel Rosa in prison, then . . . *(Beat.)* There's not a man on the committee who hasn't supported what's been happening here. (JULIO *laughs to himself.*) What has been said today cannot come as any surprise to you. We assume that by asking us . . .

JULIO: Yes. *(Pause.)* Yes. It is only the harsh tone with which one has been confronted. This was not expected. Nor is this appreciated. From such sympathetic friends. *(Beat.)* Keep the

fucking self-righteousness out of this. You aren't in Western Europe.
(Pause.)
ALBERTO: I understand. I'll talk to Hans. He just wants to get this over with, is all. You can't blame him for that. It seems so simple. Just let the guy out of prison. I mean what is the big deal? *(Beat.)* I'll talk to Hans, get him to tone down his arguments a little. *(Beat.)* But in his defense, he is the vice chairman of the committee, he has the responsibility, and the real understanding; Quinn and I, we're really just here for the . . .
JULIO: *(Suddenly turns.)* Hans Einhorn doesn't understand shit about my country. And he doesn't give a damn about human rights.
ALBERTO: That's not terribly fair, Julio.
JULIO: He's a careerist. Don't fool yourself. You only kid yourself thinking this man cares about shit. The biggest careerist writer I know. Everyone knows about him.
ALBERTO: That's not true. It's not, and you know it.
JULIO: *(To* ERNESTO*)* Aren't I right?
ERNESTO: I tried to say a simple pleasantry to Mr. Einhorn in the hall, but he looked at me like I didn't exist. I assume because I'm no one important.
JULIO: Because he's no one important. You see what the people are saying?
ALBERTO: Maybe Hans didn't hear him. Maybe he was preoccupied. We all get preoccupied.
JULIO: A revolution like ours can mean nothing to him. This is obvious.
ALBERTO: This man has a reputation; he is admired; he personally has supported countless Czech exiles in Vienna; he acts from his heart and he has a big heart; Hans Einhorn is a passionate man.
JULIO: Hans is passionate, yes, about Hans. Look at the characters he writes. Egomaniacs.
ALBERTO: I thought you hadn't read . . .
JULIO: Don't you think we know that in Europe now it's not just the work that the critics are looking at, you've got to have the correct posturing to go along with it. Einhorn is posturing, he's been posturing, and he's been getting the reviews. But I am not blaming him for this, I am just saying don't get holier-than-thou with me. I do not see why I have to sit in that room

and take the shit as this fat-ass Nazi lectures me on human rights. *(Beat.)* If he wants to talk genocide, I'll listen; that I'm sure he knows something about.

ALBERTO: Julio . . . !

JULIO: And that's why I'm not going back in there until he's gone, Alberto. *(Beat.)*

ALBERTO: Are you crazy? *(Beat.)* Julio, you know that's not possible. You have to know that.

JULIO: I don't see why that's such a big concession to make. *(Pause.)*

ALBERTO: Concession? *(Beat.)* I thought we were supposed to be airing our views. When did it become a negotiation? *(Beat.)* What's to negotiate? *(Pause.)* What's your secretary's name again?

ERNESTO: Ernesto Pico.

ALBERTO: Ernesto, go and tell Mr. Einhorn we will be a little while longer. *(Beat.)* And ask Mr. Quinn to please join us in here.

*(*ERNESTO *moves to go.)*

JULIO: I have nothing to say to Quinn. *(*ERNESTO *stops. Pause.)* Get Quinn. *(*ERNESTO *goes.)* Why not? But I think I have made my terms very clear. *(He begins to wash his face in the sink.)*

ALBERTO: Now they are "terms."

JULIO: Why can't the German just go back to the Hilton? What's the big deal?

ALBERTO: I thought you didn't call it the Hilton anymore.

JULIO: Oh right. That's true. We don't. *(Dries his face.)* How old's his wife anyway—to have a baby?

ALBERTO: She's his second wife.

JULIO: So he dumped the first. Figures.

ALBERTO: I don't know. Maybe she died. *(Beat.)* She could have died, Julio.

*(*NORTON QUINN, *a middle-aged American, and* ERNESTO *enter.)*

QUINN: Hans isn't too happy about being left alone. *(Beat.)* What is it?

ALBERTO: Julio refuses to meet anymore as long as Hans is present.

QUINN: Right.

(Beat.)

ALBERTO: He's upset.

QUINN: Right. *(Beat.)* Sorry, but we came as a group. *(He turns to go.)*

JULIO: What's more important to you — your group or what you came here to discuss?

QUINN: I don't like that question.

ALBERTO: Even if we asked him, I don't think he'd just go back to the hotel.

QUINN: No. And I don't see us asking him.

JULIO: Ernesto, call for the car to take the gentlemen away. *(Beat.)* They will be needing assistance in arranging flights back home as well.

(Long pause. No one moves. Suddenly QUINN *laughs.)*

QUINN: *(To* ALBERTO*)* We have the same publisher in New York. Do you know how many translators he's gone through? He's famous for this bullying shit.

ALBERTO: Listen to him, Norton. Just listen to him. *(Beat.)* Maybe he has a point. If all we're worried about is Hans's pride . . .

QUINN: First it'll be Hans. Then one of us. What's the point, Alberto?

ALBERTO: The point, I seem to recall — is the life of Manuel Rosa. We haven't, I hope, forgotten this.

JULIO: *(Laughs to himself.)* If this were only about Manuel Rosa.

QUINN: Wait a minute, what do you mean by that? I did not understand that.

(Pause.)

JULIO: Ask Alberto.

QUINN: He probably couldn't help Rosa even if he wanted to. (JULIO *laughs.* ERNESTO *laughs.)* He hasn't shown us shit that he can do. *(They laugh.)* I think I've had all the talk I can take for one day.

JULIO: There won't be any tomorrow.

(Pause.)

QUINN: He's bluffing. He needs us here. (JULIO *laughs really hard.)* If he wants to come back to the table, I'll be at the table; with Hans.

(He goes to the door.)

JULIO: Ernesto.

(ERNESTO *goes to the door.)*

ALBERTO: Norton. *(They stop.)* We owe Rosa's family at least the rest of the afternoon. *(Beat.)* I feel somehow we can work

through this problem. *(Beat.)* I think it is at least worth a discussion.
(Long pause.)
QUINN: *(Moving to the stall)* Excuse me, I've got to pee. *(Goes into the stall. After a moment we hear him peeing.)* So discuss. Discuss. I'm listening.

SCENE EIGHT

Projection:
PRINCIPIUM 8:
STUDY THE CLASSICS

The meeting room. Table. Chairs. Overhead fan. HANS EINHORN, *an older heavyset man, sits at the table, his hands under his chin.* BILL HOWELL *sits to one side, looking at some photographs.*

(Pause.)
HANS: I know how he works. He wants me out. *(Beat.)* The games we end up playing, Bill. It's so tiring. To a man like Julio — everything is politics. The game of politics. Even a man's life — as in this case, with Manuel Rosa. How do you argue with that? They suck you in. That's what they're after. To suck you in. *(Beat.)* I've been sucked in. *(Beat.)* Think of the energy we waste. I've dealt with him before. *(Pause.)* The world could be simpler, Bill. Hand me the water pitcher.
*(*BILL *pushes the pitcher toward* HANS, *who has taken out a small flask and is making himself a drink.)*
BILL: *(With the photos)* Beautiful child. You said — sixteen months?
HANS: In the pictures. Eighteen months now. *(*BILL *continues to look at the photos.)* How's your room at the Hilton?
BILL: I'm not at the Hilton. I'm staying with Ernesto and his family. *(*HANS *looks at him.)* Mr. Montero's secretary. *(Beat.)* We're old friends. Though it's been years since we saw each . . .
HANS: Right. *(Beat.)* My room sucks. *(Beat.)* There comes a stage

in one's life—especially if one is successful, whatever that means . . . *(Laughs to himself and sips.)* when certain seemingly trivial things can all but unsettle one. One's whole day can be affected.

(Short pause.)

BILL: I can talk to Ernesto; maybe he can do something about your room. I think he made the arrangements.

HANS: I wouldn't bother. *(Beat.)* I'm already in my third. *(Beat.)* They're all the same. *(Beat.)* When you reach my age, Bill—and you will, believe me you will—you too may wish to pamper yourself a little. Even in a country like this. Especially in a country like this. *(Laughs to himself.)* And if you can't, you end up asking yourself what the hell has one worked all these years for? *(Pause.)* I'm shocking you.

BILL: No. No, you're not.

HANS: I know what you're thinking—how can Hans Einhorn talk about his life's work as if it were all written just so he could live a little more comfortably? *(Beat.)* Don't be shocked, Bill. *(Laughs to himself.)* There's a lot to say for shocking people. I shock people all the time. I feel it's part of a writer's job. *(Beat.)* To shock.

(HANS *takes out the flask and pours another drink. Pause.* BILL *finishes looking at the photos and puts them in front of* HANS.*)*

BILL: Thank you. Very handsome child.

HANS: *(Drinking)* I write for him now. *(Taps the photos.)* Everybody should have one. Even when you're old you should have one. A child keeps you young. Keeps you thinking, Bill. We need youth. We couldn't live without it. *(Pause.)* But you, Bill—or is it William?

BILL: Bill's fine.

HANS: You, Bill, are still young. *(Laughs to himself.)* And successful. Congratulations.

BILL: Not really, Mr. Einhorn. Nothing like—

HANS: To be asked by the Writers Committee, Bill. Very nice. Very good.

BILL: Actually it was Mr. Quinn who asked me along. Unofficially. I thought everyone knew that. Everyone was supposed to be told that. *(Pause.* HANS *nods and looks away.)* Mr. Quinn had read some of my pieces. *(Pause.* HANS *nods while looking away. He puts the photos back in his pocket.)* You must be very proud. *(*HANS *turns to him.)* About your son, I mean.

HANS: My wife is. *(He laughs to himself at this private joke. Looks to* BILL *)* I enjoyed your book, Bill.

BILL: Which book, Mr. Einhorn?

HANS: Which book? *(Beat.)* You are supposed to say "Thank you." Or "How nice." I don't know which book. I don't know any book, Bill, I thought you were old enough to understand that. I thought you were old enough to have this conversation with me. *(Pause.)* Grow up, son.

(ERNESTO enters with a coffee tray.)

ERNESTO: Comrade Julio thought we might enjoy a little coffee. *(Sets down the tray.)*

HANS: He thinks I'm getting drunk.

(Pause. ERNESTO *pours coffee.)*

BILL: Ernesto . . .

ERNESTO: Cream, Bill? *(They look at each other.)*

BILL: Thank you. Thank you very much, Ernesto.

HANS: The first time I came up against him was in Vienna. There was a conference. When isn't there a conference? *(Laughs to himself.)* Yes. Yes. *(Beat.)* Julio had nothing then. He wasn't Minister of Culture. He hadn't even a country to be Minister of Culture of. Nothing. *(Nods toward* ERNESTO.*)* Like him, Bill. No older than him. And Julio stands up — and he starts making demands. This is true. He wants this person made president of the conference, that person treasurer. We all just look at each other. Heinrich Böll is sitting almost next to me — and there is a man with a social conscience; if anyone's got one it is this man. It was this man. And Böll is saying — who is this boy with his demands? What are we: writers or terrorists? What are we: writers or revolutionaries? We are going to have to decide! So Julio says he wouldn't talk until Böll has left the room. *(Pause.)* You see he does this all the time. He has his tactics. *(Beat.)* You learn to expect it. I know what they're talking about in there. *(Beat.)* Böll didn't leave. *(Beat.)* He asked our fellow writers if they wanted him to leave. Writers have to put their foot down sometime. If we don't, who will? *(Pours himself another drink.)* Who will?

(HANS drinks. ALBERTO, QUINN, *and* JULIO *enter.)*

HANS: Bathroom break over so soon? *(Pause. They all sit down.)* Well?

ALBERTO: Let's get back to our discussion, can we? I think I will have some of that coffee, if you don't mind, Bill.

(BILL *passes the coffee.*)
HANS: Back to our discussions? *(He laughs.)* Very good. Very good. How nice to see our host come to his senses. Don't think I don't know what's been going on.
ALBERTO: Hans . . .
HANS: *(To* JULIO*)* You have come to your senses, haven't you? *(Laughs; to* ALBERTO *and* QUINN:*)* I want to thank you both. Thank you. I appreciate the support. Now if we can, getting back to the case of Mr. Manuel Rosa . . .
ALBERTO: Hans . . .
HANS: I'll call on you in a moment, Alberto. I have a few thoughts of my own which I wish to convey to Mr. . . .
ALBERTO: Hans. *(*HANS *looks at him.)* Norton is going to chair the meeting for the rest of the day.
(Pause. HANS, *realizing the compromise made in the bathroom, looks first at* ALBERTO, *then to* QUINN. *He stands and moves away.)*
HANS: Fuck you.
ALBERTO: I'm sorry. Norton.
HANS: Fuck you!!!
JULIO: *(Pointing to* HANS*)* May I just say to Mr. Einhorn that I had nothing to . . .
NORTON: No! I'm running this meeting now.
ALBERTO: Wait. You had nothing to do with what?
JULIO: With Norton being made chair of the meeting.
NORTON: Alberto . . .
ALBERTO: That's outrageous. How can you say that?
JULIO: It was your idea. Not mine.
ALBERTO: You wanted him out!
HANS: *(To* BILL*)* What did I tell you?
JULIO: I only want the record to show that it was Alberto Fava who connived to have Quinn take over the chair. That is only the truth, is it not?
ERNESTO: *(Writing)* I'm writing that down.
JULIO: I had nothing to do with your humiliation, Hans.
ALBERTO: It was not meant as a humiliation.
JULIO: But that's how he's taken it. Haven't you?
HANS: Perhaps you'd really like me to leave.
QUINN: No!!!
(Beat.)
JULIO: *(Under his breath)* Ask me.
QUINN: Shut up. *(Pause.)* Sit down, Hans. Sit down, Hans!

(HANS *sits down.*)

JULIO: Yes. And show us the pictures of your baby again.

QUINN: Alberto . . .

ALBERTO: Norton, please. Please!

(Beat.)

QUINN: Okay. I believe I was still speaking just before we took our break.

HANS: You were still speaking as Julio walked out of the room, yes.

(Beat.)

QUINN: *(Looks at his notes.)* Uh-huh. *(Looks up.)* Julio, what I personally cannot quite understand is why are you doing this to yourself. I'm talking about Rosa now. It doesn't make any sense to me — political sense — to imprison a man like Manuel Rosa. He can't do any real harm on the outside. For one he's too old and second who's going to listen to him? *(Beat.)* His credibility is questionable after all. In fact, it is only this imprisonment that gives him any credibility at all. So you see, it seems to me that the only real damage he can cause you is by staying in prison. You understand what I am saying?

JULIO: Rosa is a criminal.

QUINN: Maybe. That is not the point of my question.

JULIO: It is the point of his imprisonment though.

QUINN: What I mean is — his books, Julio, they happen to be very well thought of.

JULIO: I don't understand what that means to this.

QUINN: The books are considered good. He's good. *(Beat.)* A good poet, I mean.

JULIO: And if he were a bad poet, then he would deserve prison? *(Turns to* ERNESTO.*)* What is this, some sort of justice by literary criticism?

*(*ERNESTO *smiles.)*

HANS: *(To* ALBERTO*)* He shouldn't be trying to reason with him.

ALBERTO: Hans . . .

HANS: Why don't you just come out and ask him what he wants in exchange for releasing Rosa. Why waste our . . .

QUINN: Hans, shut up! *(Beat.)* I didn't call on you.

HANS: You didn't call on . . .

ALBERTO: *(Yells.)* He said he didn't call on you!!! *(He raises a finger to be called on.)*

QUINN: Alberto.

HANS: You two a club now?
ALBERTO: Julio, stand back for a moment if you can and try to see how it looks. It may not be how it really is—but appearances can as well have the power of truth; as any of us well knows. I mean—take the fact that we are here. Why would Norton, Hans, and myself come here?
JULIO: I'm sure you have your reasons. I told you in the bathroom what I thought Hans's reasons were.
HANS: Which are?
JULIO: You need the posturing to keep getting the reviews.
ALBERTO: Hans, ignore him. *(Beat.)* We are here because Rosa is a writer. People, many, many, people, Julio, have come to be quite sensitive about countries which arrest their writers. It is seen as a sign. A symbol meaning more than it may in fact be meant to mean. *(Beat.)* And people take that symbol and they use it to define for themselves their feelings, their impressions about the whole country. Call this unfair—and no doubt it is in some cases, just as it is very fair in many others—but fair or unfair aside this is just what happens. *(Beat.)* Let's say right now for the sake of argument that Manuel Rosa is a real criminal.
JULIO: Of course he is. And not just for the sake of . . .
ALBERTO: Julio, sometimes necessity demands us to release one criminal so that a whole country will not be accused of the wrong crimes. There are people prone to use Rosa not because they wish to help him, but because through him they can disparage your country and all your country has been able to achieve in its short life; all your country represents. *(Beat.)* It is not our wish to see this happen. *(Beat.)* Norton was telling us that a magazine in the States—it's a new magazine, literary and aesthetic, but very conservative in outlook, and naturally quite political in a very subtle way—this magazine is planning on starting a new award. A literary award. The whole point of this award is so they can give it to Rosa. *(Beat.)* You see specifically how he will be used. You see just how your revolution will be victimized. Julio, what is the point? Say he served his full sentence. Say he's ill. Everyone will believe that such an old man is ill.
(Pause.)
QUINN: *(Quietly)* Let him out—if you can—Julio. And if you can't . . . *(He shrugs.)*

(Long pause. JULIO *stands, moves away.)*
JULIO: *(Nodding)* Ernesto . . .
ERNESTO: I don't know what you are all talking about. Manuel Rosa is not in prison. We have no prisons in our country.
ALBERTO: *(Banging the table)* Julio!!!!!
ERNESTO: *(After a beat)* But if—and I repeat if—the Minister of Justice can be convinced to let Manuel Rosa leave our country, he is going to want to know what will we receive in return?
BILL: Ernesto?
QUINN: *(To* BILL*)* Sh-sh.
HANS: Didn't I say we just should have asked?
QUINN: We'd hoped we could convince you on humanitarian grounds.
JULIO: What humanitarian grounds? I haven't heard any humanitarian grounds.
(Pause.)
QUINN: *(Finally)* There is nothing we have to give—that I can think of.
ERNESTO: *(Opening a folder)* There is a young man—one of ours—presently in prison in Honduras. An excellent poet. Comrade Julio as president of our Writers Union and as Minister of Culture has repeatedly asked for this man's release. Perhaps if you could . . .
QUINN: Of course. Of course. That is what we are about. Look, we are interested in hearing about any cases. If you don't tell us, then we can't help. What's the name.
ERNESTO: *(After a beat)* José Dorio.
QUINN: *(Writes it down.)* José Dorio. We'll wire London in the morning. I'm sure they'll come up with something they can do.
HANS: José Dorio? *(*ERNESTO *nods.)* Hasn't the Committee been informed about him already?
JULIO: Yes.
QUINN: There must have been some . . .
HANS: I seem to recall that no proof could be found that this Dorio had ever written a line of poetry in his life. The Hondurans, I believe, even went so far as to claim he was illiterate.
ERNESTO: He is illiterate. *(Beat.)* That is true. *(Beat.)* But since we want him released, we call him a poet. *(Pause.)* If your organization would support us in this claim . . .

QUINN: I don't think . . . Julio I'm sorry, we . . . I don't believe this. What's your name?
BILL: It's Ernesto. Ernesto Pico.
QUINN: Ernesto, I don't know where you got the idea that we could just proclaim someone a writer. That is, it's . . . I don't know. That is not what we do.
BILL: I think Ernesto was being ironic, Mr. Quinn.
QUINN: *(To ERNESTO)* Is that true?
ERNESTO: If Bill says so.
(Pause.)
QUINN: Oh. *(Beat.)* Oh.
JULIO: Actually I thought Ernesto was speaking theoretically. Is it that much harder for a committee such as yours to proclaim an illiterate a writer than a criminal innocent?
QUINN: Julio, Rosa's a political prisoner.
JULIO: What does that mean?
QUINN: His crimes are only political.
JULIO: So is José Dorio's illiteracy. And if one can blind oneself to political crimes why not also to political illiteracy? *(Beat.)* And now that José Dorio is no longer illiterate in our eyes, it is not much more trouble to see him also as a poet. And in regard to Mr. Quinn's earlier distinction regarding imprisoned good writers and not so good ones, I believe Ernesto would also ask us to think of José Dorio not only as a mere poet, but as one of distinction and great critical acclaim. *(Beat.)* Perhaps this is the point Ernesto was trying to make.
(Long pause.)
HANS: May I . . . ?
QUINN: No. *(Pause.)* Don't misunderstand me—we don't wish to soft-pedal the difficulties you people have had to go through. You have to just believe me when I say I have all the respect in the world for what this country has been attempting.
HANS: He's so sincere.
QUINN: Also—I can only imagine how a man like Rosa—who chose to be a part of that government and, as you have suggested, may have written the occasional speech for that government—what he must mean to you. *(Beat.)* But my point is this—what Rosa did, well it wasn't exactly like he was here torturing people himself. He wasn't even in the country.
JULIO: He was the government's Ambassador to Spain.
QUINN: That is my point. We are not talking about a war crimi-

nal here, are we? What this is, is political. I want that made very clear. I wouldn't be here if he were a war criminal.

HANS: Who said he was a war criminal?

QUINN: *(To* JULIO*)* You're not questioning that?

JULIO: No.

QUINN: Good, because I wanted that perfectly clear.
(Pause.)

HANS: What's all that about?
*(*ALBERTO *shrugs.)*

QUINN: Now . . . *(Opens another file.)*

JULIO: But this does not mean that Manuel Rosa bears no responsibility for his government's actions. He did choose to join such a government.

QUINN: To be Ambassador to Spain. I'm told he always wanted to live in Spain.

ALBERTO: True. You know his work on Don Quixote.

JULIO: You make him into a very stupid man when you say something like that. *(Beat.)* What you may not be understanding, gentlemen, is what such a government that we had could be like. This I am not sure you understand. Though maybe it is something you can never understand.

ALBERTO: Don't start, Julio. You are not the only persecuted man in this room.

JULIO: Persecuted, yes. I am sure you have been persecuted, Alberto. *(Pats him on the shoulder.)*

ALBERTO: Don't patronize.

JULIO: I only think that having the police follow you around and give you parking tickets or—in Quinn's case—what is the worst, Norton—having your taxes audited?

BILL: Mr. Montero.

JULIO: *(Ignoring him)* There is a difference, that is all I am saying. There is this understanding gap, shall we call it. You talk about how a few fickle people out there may get the wrong impression about my country, when what is most important, is it not, is that the people here, my own people, get the right impression of what we are all about. This is what matters to me. There is much you will never comprehend—you can begin by what we all have had to live through.
(Beat.)

BILL: Mr. Montero. Excuse me.

QUINN: Bill, sit down.

BILL: No. I was here during that time. I do know what you are talking about. Ernesto can tell you.

(ERNESTO *says nothing.*)

QUINN: That's right, Bill, you wrote about that experience didn't you? Sit down, please.

HANS: I didn't read that book.

BILL: Wait. I want to show you. You want to see — I'll show you. *(He takes down his pants.)* Ernesto, take off your shirt. Take it off.

(ERNESTO *looks at* JULIO, *who shrugs;* ERNESTO *begins to take off his shirt.*)

BILL: *(To the others)* Look here. There. They used this metal wire, like a cattle prod. I found out later that's what it was like. Like a cattle prod. And look at his back. *(Pointing out wounds on* ERNESTO's *back)* There. You have pins in there now, don't you? (ERNESTO *nods.*) Look at that!

(There is a long embarrassed silence. The others have only glanced at the wounds.)

BILL: What's wrong? *(Beat.)* I wanted Mr. Montero to know that he wasn't the only one. Isn't that what you were trying to say, Mr. Fava? *(Beat.)* I do know what it's like.

JULIO: I guess you do.

(Beat.)

QUINN: For Christ sake, please pull up your pants, Bill.

(BILL *does.* ERNESTO *puts his shirt back on.*)

BILL: I don't understand.

QUINN: Bill, we're talking. Where were we?

JULIO: I don't know.

(ALBERTO *raises a finger.*)

QUINN: What Alberto?

ALBERTO: *(Without looking up)* My wife was tortured. Just last year. The fascists wanted me. They cut with a knife across here. *(Points across the breast.)* They also used cigarettes. *(Beat.)* They . . . *(Points to* BILL *and* ERNESTO.) reminded me of it. *(Pause.)*

HANS: I read the piece you wrote about that. Very moving.

ALBERTO: Thank you.

(Pause.)

QUINN: Okay — where were we?

SCENE NINE

Projection:
PRINCIPIUM 9:
WORK WITHIN YOUR LIMITS

The porch of ERNESTO'*s house.* BILL *and* ERNESTO *sit on two rusted lawn chairs. A child's tricycle in a corner. Crickets. Evening. Pause.*

ERNESTO: Tell me more.
BILL: Why?
ERNESTO: Bill, do I have to have a reason? What is the matter with you? *(*BILL *looks at him.)* What's wrong? *(Short pause.)* I'm your friend, remember?
BILL: *(Turns away and continues.)* The book, it sort of set me off as an article writer. Can't keep up with the demand really; people want to send me all over the world.
ERNESTO: That's wonderful, Bill. I envy you.
BILL: You know, I can't tell if you're being sincere or not.
ERNESTO: Why wouldn't I be sincere? I don't understand. *(Beat.)* Bill, really it is not me who's been acting strange.
BILL: Right. Right. *(Beat.)* Sorry. *(Continues.)* Funny how you plan things and then . . .
ERNESTO: Then what?
BILL: Then something, like what happened to us, happens and it changes everything. It changed everything—eventually. *(Beat.)*
ERNESTO: I don't quite understand, Bill. *(*BILL *looks at him.)* Come on, why do you keep looking at me like that?
BILL: Like what? *(Beat.)* Forget it. *(Continuing)* I am saying that I wouldn't be writing articles if I hadn't written that book and I wouldn't have written that book if . . . if it hadn't happened. That's what I mean, so that's what my advice to someone would be now—don't plan. Because why bother, everything is going to change anyway so what's the point, you'll only get yourself frustrated. I was getting myself frustrated until I realized that.

ERNESTO: I see what you are saying now. Yes. That is very, very interesting.
(Pause.)
BILL: You son of a bitch, will you stop that! And don't say stop what, you know what I mean. What's happened to you?
ERNESTO: What's happened to you?
BILL: Why do I feel that everything you say to me is a lie? It is driving me crazy—all this lying, Ernesto. The reason I came down here was to see you. The whole committee thing gave me the chance, but I came to see you.
ERNESTO: Ah. *(Beat.)* Julio mentioned to me something about how you'd been commissioned to do an article on Norton Quinn. I thought that's what you were doing down here. Working on your article about Norton Quinn.
BILL: I'm doing that too. *(Beat.)* I would have come . . .
ERNESTO: Who's lying now, Bill? *(Pause.)* I asked you, who's . . . (BILL *gets up and moves away.*) I thought it went okay today. People got their points across. *(Beat.)* We'll have to see what happens tomorrow.
BILL: I thought we agreed we wouldn't talk about . . . I thought we wanted to hear about each other. *(Pause.)*
ERNESTO: I'm sure you figured out that we planned all that about the illiterate poet. We even rehearsed it. We didn't know Quinn. Sort of took a flyer on him by making him chairman, you see we didn't know how he'd . . .
BILL: Ernesto . . .
ERNESTO: "Bendable," that's the word. You understand. *(Beat.)* But tomorrow's another day. Julio's thinking of demanding that Einhorn become chairman again. *(Laughs.)* If you can have him removed why not also have him put back? That makes the point, I guess, doesn't it? I guess maybe I shouldn't be telling you all this.
BILL: You know what you're doing.
ERNESTO: Excuse me? *(Beat.)* Sometimes friends bring out of one more than they wish to say.
BILL: Right. *(Laughs.)* Excuse me, Ernesto, but I think I would like to go to bed now. It has been a tiring—draining—day.
ERNESTO: I hope you haven't been disappointed? *(Beat.)* In me? *(Beat.)* Is it in me? Or in you? *(He puts something in* BILL's *hand.)*
BILL: What's this?
ERNESTO: Your hotel room key.

BILL: But I thought I was staying . . .
ERNESTO: My wife and I thought you'd be more comfortable . . .
BILL: Oh. *(Beat.)* I see. It doesn't look so good having an American in your . . .
ERNESTO: My wife and I thought you'd be more comfortable . . .
BILL: *(Suddenly yells.)* Bullshit!!!!!! *(Pause.)* Please. Ernesto, I do understand. Just don't bullshit me. Not me. Okay? Not me. *(He turns and starts to go.)*
ERNESTO: I'm not bullshitting.
BILL: *(Suddenly turns back.)* Fuck you!!!!! *(Pause as they look at each other.)*
ERNESTO: Bill, they can't complain if you happen to fall asleep on the couch.
BILL: Are you sure? *(Beat.)*
ERNESTO: No. No, I'm not.
BILL: Then I don't want to . . .
ERNESTO: Do you want to stay?
BILL: Ernesto?
ERNESTO: Do you want to stay? You can stay here if you want. We would like you to stay. *(Pause.* BILL *sits back down.)*
BILL: What are you writing?
ERNESTO: Nothing. *(Beat.)* A poem. A long poem. *(Gestures out.)* A natural history of that countryside. Flowers. Trees. Birds.
BILL: Any gannets?
ERNESTO: What's a gannet? *(Beat.)* No. No gannets. Sorry.
BILL: We were so stupid then.
ERNESTO: Not stupid.
BILL: Young then. Young!
ERNESTO: Yes. We were young.
BILL: And silly. The things we thought. *(Beat.)* We were stupid.
ERNESTO: Right. *(Beat.)* Right. We were.

SCENE TEN

Projection:
PRINCIPIUM 10:
MAKE IT NEW

1970. A courtyard of the prison. Bright sun. ERNESTO *and* BILL *sit, tied to posts, at a distance from each other. They are blindfolded.*

(A few shots of gunfire from another section of the courtyard — at some distance.)

ERNESTO: *(Twisting his body toward* BILL.*)* Bill?

BILL: I'm here. *(Pause.)*

ERNESTO: And then what happens? *(Pause.)*

BILL: Robert decides it is just time he put his foot down, so he tells his father. He tells him that if he is ever going to do anything, it is not going to be in St. Louis.

ERNESTO: Yeh.

BILL: But, Ernesto, what his father hears is that Robert, whom he calls Bobby just to put him down — that I make very clear in my novel. That "Bobby" is his father's way of putting him down. *(Beat.)* In the manuscript I underline "Bobby." To make this clear. *(Beat.)* When it's printed it'll be in italics.

(Another set of gunshots, which sound closer.)

ERNESTO: Bill?

BILL: I'm still here. *(Beat.)* I think they're getting closer. I think they are like coming down a line. *(Beat.)* They fake it to frighten you. I heard that somewhere. *(Beat.)* Shit, I will bet you anything he's already getting telegrams.

ERNESTO: Who is getting telegrams?

BILL: The general. His people are getting telegrams. About us, Ernesto. *(Beat.)* Someone's sending telegrams. *(Beat.)* My parents are sending telegrams. *(Long pause. A dog barks in the distance.)* They just laugh at him, Ernesto.

ERNESTO: Who?

BILL: Robert's parents. In my book. When Robert tells his parents that he has to get out of St. Louis before his brain blows up they just laugh at him. And when his father—he teaches economics at a local university—when he asks Robert just how he plans to live, Robert finally confesses that he hopes to be a musician. He plays the bass. He had a group. They broke up the previous winter, but he did at least have the experience of having a group. It wasn't so foolish as they thought, Ernesto.

ERNESTO: No. It doesn't sound foolish to me, Bill.

BILL: Thank you. So he runs away without telling them exactly where he is going. Fuck them, he thinks.

(Another round of gunfire.)

ERNESTO: Bill?!!

BILL: *(Loudly)* But they come after him! There's a whole chapter just about this chase. This escape. *(Beat.)* It's written all in one sentence. The entire chapter is one very long sentence. With a lot of parentheses. *(Beat. Almost yells.)* So he escapes!!

ERNESTO: Good for him. *(BILL begins to break down. ERNESTO twists toward him again.)*

BILL: I'm all right. I'm all right.

ERNESTO: I'm hugging you. Do you feel me hugging you?

BILL: Yes. *(Beat.)* Ernesto? *(ERNESTO tries to turn.)* And you said they wouldn't use the machine on my cock.

(Pause.)

ERNESTO: Hey Bill, we're writers right? And people are always sending telegrams to get writers out. Other writers are always sending telegrams to get other writers out. Hug me back. Thank you.

(Beat.)

BILL: His father, Ernesto, just could not understand him. He would not even try to understand him. Shit!

ERNESTO: I'm sorry.

BILL: Robert was suffocating. His soul cries out for new places. New people. Things are changing and he wants to be a part of that. He's dying to be a part of that. He wants to matter, Ernesto. And his father will not understand that!

ERNESTO: No. No.

BILL: He isn't a kid anymore. He isn't some kid. He has things to do. He fucking has things to do! *(A soldier enters with a revolver.)*

SOLDIER: ¡Callense ahorales troca a listedes! [Shut up. You're next.]

ERNESTO: ¿Qué vas a hacer con nosotros? [What are you going to do to us?]

SOLDIER: Cállate y di tus oraciones, chiquito. Voy a contar hasta diez. [Shut up and say your prayers, sonny boy. I will count to ten.]

ERNESTO: He said—he will count to . . .

BILL: Okay. Okay.

SOLDIER: ¡Tu también, Americano! [You too, American.] *(He pushes* BILL *with his gun.)* Uno. Dos. Tres. Cuatro. Cinco. Seis. Siete. Ocho. Nueve. *(Beat.)* Diez.

(He raises his gun in the air and shoots a single shot in the air. He looks at them, laughs to himself and walks off. Pause.)

ERNESTO: Bill?!!!

BILL: I'm still here.

(Pause.)

END

BETWEEN EAST AND WEST

For H. and L.

Between East and West was first performed on January 14, 1985 at the Yale Repertory Theatre, New Haven (Lloyd Richards, Artistic Director), with the following cast and creative contributors:

GREGOR HASEK — Thomas Hill
ERNA HASEK — Jo Henderson

Director — John Madden
Set designer — Basha Zmyslowska
Costume designer — Rusty Smith
Lighting designer — David Alan Stach
Sound designer — James Brewcsynski
Stage manager — Margaret Adair

Between East and West was subsequently presented on December 10, 1987 at the Hampstead Theatre Club, London, with the following cast:

GREGOR HASEK — John Woodvine
ERNA HASEK — Sheila Allen

Director — David Jones
Set designer — Eileen Diss
Costume designer — Sue Plummer
Lighting designer — Mick Hughes
Sound designer — Colin Brown
Dialect coach — Joan Washington
Stage managers — Catherine Bailey, Caroline Beale, Nick Frankfort, and Hedda Moore

THE CHARACTERS

GREGOR and ERNA HASEK, Czech emigrés in their fifties. He is a stage and film director; she, an actress.

NOTE

When Gregor and Erna are speaking "English," they speak with strong accents and in a somewhat unconfident way. When they speak "Czech," they have either very little or no accents. In the text, the "English" lines are capitalized.

THE SETTING

A one-room apartment, sparsely furnished, on the upper East Side, New York City.

THE TIME

1983.

THE TITLES

The TITLE given each scene should be projected all the time the scene is played and should remain in view for a few moments after the scene is over.

THE SCENES

One: THE CULMINATION
Two: EIGHT MONTHS EARLIER
Three: THE CONTEXT
Four: BEFORE
Five: AND AFTER
Six: DUSTIN HOFFMAN
Seven: THE LAND OF OPPORTUNITY
Eight: BY THE BOOTSTRAPS
Nine: SHADOWS
Ten: THE FREE WORLD
Eleven: GOING PLACES
Twelve: SIBERIA
Thirteen: HIS MEMORY
Fourteen: HER MEMORY
Fifteen: SIBERIA CONTINUED
Sixteen: A FEW DAYS BEFORE
Seventeen: ERNA RECALLS AN EARLIER SCENE
Eighteen: THE CULMINATION ENDS
Nineteen: BETWEEN EAST AND WEST

SCENE ONE

Title:
THE CULMINATION

ERNA *sits watching television. She smokes.*

TELEVISION: "Shouting over the cat-calls of back benchers, Mrs. Thatcher today restated her support for the deployment of American Pershing missiles on British soil. While she spoke to Parliament, an estimated crowd of one hundred thousand Britons staged what is being described as the largest political demonstration since the war. . . ."
(The door to the hallway opens and GREGOR *enters. He wears a winter hat and coat.* ERNA *turns to him.)*
TELEVISION: "Mrs. Thatcher never referred to the Grenada invasion which has greatly strained relations with the Reagan White House. Instead she . . ."
*(*ERNA *has gotten up and turns off the television. Pause.)*
GREGOR: Do you want to tell me what you meant last night on the phone?
(She doesn't respond. He takes off his hat and coat.)
ERNA: You didn't have to come, Gregor.
GREGOR: I came.
ERNA: What about rehearsals?
GREGOR: They changed the schedule. We'll rehearse tonight. *(Pause.)* I have to catch the next train back.
ERNA: When is the next train back?
GREGOR: One hour.
ERNA: You came back for one hour? How much does the train cost?
GREGOR: Erna, I came. *(Pause.)* Erna, last night —.

ERNA: I'll bet your American actors love you. Actors always love you. I loved you.
GREGOR: Erna, last night you scared me.
ERNA: I'm scared myself.
GREGOR: What about? *(No response.)* I will be back in two weeks.
ERNA: You won't come back.
GREGOR: That's a stupid thing to say and you know it.
ERNA: I know it's stupid. Yes.
(Short pause.)
GREGOR: You don't have the heat on in here, do you? I'll get you a sweater.
(He moves to the closet.)
ERNA: You can't just let things slip away, Gregor.
GREGOR: What's slipping away?
(He gets the sweater.)
ERNA: Gregor . . .
(He stops.)
ERNA: They will take and they won't stop. The moment you give, they take. That's how it is in a country like this.
GREGOR: What do you have against this country anyway?
ERNA: I don't have anything against it. And I don't have anything for it. That's only the way you think, not me. But you won't understand that.
(Pause.)
GREGOR: You've been alone too long.
ERNA: Just three weeks.
GREGOR: Why don't you come to Hartford with me.
ERNA: And sit in a hotel room? I'm sitting in this room.
GREGOR: You can watch rehearsals. You'll be treated very well. They'll adore you.
ERNA: Like they adore you.
GREGOR: Erna — what I'm doing is a job! Try to understand that — it's nothing more!
ERNA: I don't want to see you give up.
GREGOR: What have I given up?! What the hell do I have to give up?!!!
ERNA: You don't know.
GREGOR: Erna — would you like to talk to a doctor?
ERNA: A doctor? Oh that's right. In the West that's what you do, isn't it? Talk to a doctor. *(Pause.)* I'd better pack.
GREGOR: You'll come to Hartford? *(Pause.)* When?

ERNA: I'd better pack.

GREGOR: Come tomorrow. There's a train at ten. I'll make sure someone meets you. I'll talk to the stage manager. Erna . . .

(She has turned away.)

GREGOR: It'll make us both feel better, I'm sure of it.

(He puts his coat on, goes to kiss her — she doesn't respond.)

ERNA: I'm glad — you're sure of it.

GREGOR: *(At the door)* We'll go out to eat. What kind of food would you like? There's a very good Japanese restaurant near the theater . . .

ERNA: Japanese? Yes. That would make sense for two Czechs in America.

(He goes. She turns the television back on.)

TELEVISION: "The opposition Social Democratic Party, ignoring an appeal by former Chancellor Helmut Schmidt, said today that it could not accept the deployment of American medium-range missiles in West Germany. The decision, taken at a special party congress in Cologne, was the culmination of . . ."

SCENE TWO

Title:
EIGHT MONTHS EARLIER

The apartment eight months earlier. The day after GREGOR *and* ERNA's *arrival in America. The apartment has a few less things; also, there is no television.* GREGOR *has just entered and is taking off his jacket.* ERNA *fusses in the kitchen.*

GREGOR: It's not at all what I expected. I expected it to be different of course, but not this different.

ERNA: How different?

GREGOR: How different did I expect it? Or how different is it?

ERNA: Whichever makes you happy, Gregor.

GREGOR: You're really not interested, are you? You know, I can't understand that, Erna.

ERNA: Who said I'm not interested?
GREGOR: It's obvious.
ERNA: Gregor, I'm interested.
GREGOR: No you're not.
ERNA: I'm listening aren't I? You were saying New York is so different.
(Pause.)
GREGOR: It's nothing like Prague, Erna.
ERNA: There's only one Prague.
GREGOR: You really should have come with me. It's hard to put into words. The second I walked out onto the sidewalk I could feel it. You want to know where I went?
ERNA: Where did you go, Gregor?
GREGOR: I went into the subway. I bought a token—they don't have tickets—tokens. And I waited for a train—you can travel as far as you want on one token.
ERNA: Really?
GREGOR: And a train pulled in. In fact, two. One going in each direction.
ERNA: Did you know where you were going?
GREGOR: No. I didn't understand the map.
ERNA: But you got on the train?
GREGOR: I wanted to, Erna. I wanted to go to the end of the line. To get out where the blacks live. I wanted to see that. You don't see that in Prague.
ERNA: You don't see what?
GREGOR: A whole section of blacks. You see pictures. We've seen pictures, Erna.
ERNA: What pictures?
GREGOR: Of black sections in New York City! *(Beat.)* Well, I've seen these pictures.
ERNA: So have I, Gregor.
GREGOR: So then I wanted to see for myself what it was like.
ERNA: And what was it like?
GREGOR: Erna, I do not think that is a strange thing to want to see on your first day in New York.
ERNA: Strange? Why would it be strange? It's what I would want to do. We've heard so much about those places. *(Beat.)* We've seen pictures.
GREGOR: That's true.
ERNA: So what was it like?

GREGOR: The black sections?
ERNA: Yes.
GREGOR: I never got there. I never actually got on the train.
ERNA: You never got on the train?
GREGOR: No. I wanted to. But I didn't. I let the train leave. I stayed on the platform.
ERNA: I see.
GREGOR: I didn't know where they were going.
ERNA: Oh.
GREGOR: I tried to ask a black man who was standing on the platform, but my English I guess is not so good as I thought.
ERNA: Your English is very good, Gregor. My English isn't very good.
GREGOR: In any case, he didn't seem to understand.
ERNA: I see, so you stayed on the platform all this time?
GREGOR: No. I went back onto the street and walked up Fifth Avenue. And I bought some cigarettes.

(He takes out two packs.)

ERNA: Kents? You bought Kents?
GREGOR: For one dollar each.
ERNA: Each cigarette?
GREGOR: Each of these packages, Erna. For one dollar each.
ERNA: Only one dollar for American cigarettes. For Kents?
GREGOR: This is America, Erna . . . I bought the cigarettes and I bought an umbrella.

(He shows her a black umbrella.)

ERNA: It was raining? From up here it didn't look like it was raining.
GREGOR: I bought it from a boy on the street. I could have also bought a watch. But I just bought the umbrella. See here—it has a button. *(Presses the button and the umbrella opens.)* And I went into the Plaza Hotel carrying the umbrella.
ERNA: You just walked in? Gregor, are you sure you can do that?
GREGOR: The doorman opened the door for me so I went in.
ERNA: What did you do in the hotel?
GREGOR: I went out again. Though I went out before he could open the door for me. He was busy opening the car door for a millionaire.
ERNA: For who?
GREGOR: A millionaire.
ERNA: How did you find out this man was a millionaire?

GREGOR: If you'd seen him, you'd know. I told you you should have come with me.

ERNA: I know. I will.

GREGOR: And Erna, across the street is the park and at the corner of this park were bums. Don't ask me how I knew they were bums, it was obvious. One had a plastic bag over his foot.

ERNA: Really?

GREGOR: So here was this millionaire and here was this bum. Both right there together. I guess that's democracy.

ERNA: A bum and a millionaire are democracy?

GREGOR: You know what I mean. I wanted to talk to the bum so I went up to him.

ERNA: What did you say?

GREGOR: Nothing. I never actually talked to him.

ERNA: Maybe the next time.

GREGOR: Yes.

ERNA: When you're more comfortable with English.

GREGOR: Yes. Then we can ask anybody anything.

ERNA: Not anything, Gregor.

GREGOR: What can't we ask, Erna?

ERNA: I don't know yet.

GREGOR: Then we can ask anybody anything.

ERNA: I guess so. But still be careful.

GREGOR: I'm always careful.

ERNA: That's not true.

GREGOR: Erna, can't we go one day without bringing that up, please?

(Pause.)

ERNA: So what did you do after you didn't speak to the bum?

GREGOR: What would you have done?

ERNA: What would I have done? I think I would have bought another package of Kents.

(He takes out another pack of Kents. They look at each other and break out laughing.)

ERNA: *(Through the laughter)* Next time I'll go too.

SCENE THREE

Title:
THE CONTEXT

ERNA *alone at the table, reading* The New York Times. *To her side are three dictionaries—a Czech/English-English/Czech; a Czech; and an English. She refers to these often. She smokes and drinks coffee as she reads. Even though it is morning, she has been up for quite awhile and is dressed.*

ERNA: *(In a loud voice, reading)* "IS REAGAN'S FOREIGN POLICY OVERHEATED OR WARMING UP?" *(She pronounces "Reagan" as "Regan.")* What is this "OVERHEATED OR WARMING UP?" Is it like a joke?
GREGOR: *(Off, from the bathroom)* Is what like a joke?
ERNA: "IS REAGAN'S FOREIGN POLICY OVERHEATED OR WARMING UP?" I don't understand.
GREGOR: *(Entering from the bathroom, unshaven and in his bathrobe)* It's Reagan, not Regan. Regan's some other important official. The exchequer, I think. *(He goes to the stove, takes a coffee mug.)* What don't you understand?
ERNA: The joke. "OVERHEATED OR WARMING UP."
GREGOR: *(Putting hot water into his mug)* Why is that a joke?
(He goes to the refrigerator.)
ERNA: That's what I'm asking. Is it a joke—a play on words?
GREGOR: *(With his head in the refrigerator)* I wouldn't call American foreign policy just a play on words, Erna.
(He takes an egg out of the refrigerator.)
ERNA: The headline, not the policy. I'll look it up myself.
(She begins to go through the dictionary. He starts to cook his egg.)
GREGOR: Josef was telling me last night that outside of New York City nearly everyone thinks like Ronald Reagan.
ERNA: *(Going through the dictionary)* Did he say why?
GREGOR: He said that in New York City they don't think like him at all. Because here everyone's a Democrat.
ERNA: Oh. *(Pause.)* Is Josef a Democrat?
GREGOR: I didn't want to ask.

ERNA: Why didn't you want to ask?
GREGOR: I didn't know if I should, Erna. Outside of New York City are the farms. Though there are the steel mills in the west, too.
ERNA: Certainly the steelworkers are Democrats, Gregor.
GREGOR: Steelworkers are usually socialists, Erna. *(Pause.)* It's like a car.
ERNA: What is?
GREGOR: "OVERHEATED OR WARMING UP."
ERNA: Like a car?? Oh. I see.
(She puts away the dictionary.)
GREGOR: When a car runs too long it gets overheated, but when you start it up. . . .
ERNA: I said—I understand now, Gregor.
(He shrugs. His egg has boiled, he starts to take it out.)
ERNA: *(Without looking up)* That egg in the refrigerator is bad.
(He looks at the egg.)
GREGOR: Then why was it in the refrigerator?
ERNA: *(Looking at the paper)* I was waiting for you to go shopping with me.
GREGOR: Why do you need me to take you shopping? And that doesn't explain the egg.
ERNA: I don't need you to take me shopping.
GREGOR: If you don't need me to take you, why don't you go by yourself?
ERNA: I have. *(Short pause.)* Twice.
GREGOR: So why was the bad egg in the refrigerator?
ERNA: Can't you just throw it away? *(She sets down her paper.)* I'll throw it away.
GREGOR: I can throw the egg away. *(He does.)* There, I've done it.
ERNA: How sweet of you.
(Pause.)
GREGOR: *(Looking into the refrigerator)* Is the cheese bad too?
(She shrugs without looking up.)
GREGOR: It's bad.
ERNA: There's bread. It's hard, but you can toast it. *(She gets up.)* Here. I'll toast it for you.
GREGOR: I can toast it.
(He takes out the bread, takes a large knife out of a drawer.)
ERNA: It's already sliced. It comes that way.
GREGOR: I can see that.

ERNA: Then why the knife?
GREGOR: *(Putting down the knife)* Habit.
(Pause.)
ERNA: *(Reads:)* "MR. REAGAN TRIED TO RUN OVER THE OPPOSITION WITH A HARD-LINE APPROACH." What is this "RUN OVER"?
GREGOR: *(Trying to mime it)* You know—RUN OVER.
ERNA: Oh. Like with a car again.
GREGOR: Yes.
ERNA: Americans do love their cars, don't they? Least that's what everyone always says.
GREGOR: Who's everyone, Erna?
ERNA: Don't tell me you never heard that before?
GREGOR: Of course I've heard that.
ERNA: Then the person you heard it from is one of the everyone who's always saying it.
GREGOR: But they don't say it here.
ERNA: Everyone doesn't live here, Gregor. Or have you already forgotten that?
GREGOR: I haven't forgotten anything.
ERNA: *(She turns to stare at him.)* No? *(Pause. She turns back.)* Good. *(Pause.)* You should read the paper too, Gregor, and find out what's happening in the world.
GREGOR: You mean at home? I don't need a newspaper to tell me what's happening at home.
ERNA: Oh, you're only interested in what's happening at home? Isn't what's happening here important to you too? I thought you were the one who had to live here.
GREGOR: I read the paper, damnit.
ERNA: You read a theater paper. That's not a paper.
GREGOR: I read what I need to read. We need to know certain things.
ERNA: What do we need to know that's in a theater paper?
GREGOR: Who's important—for instance.
ERNA: Oh. So who's important?
GREGOR: A million people.
ERNA: A million people can't be important—even here.
GREGOR: *(Throws up his hands.)* For example Dustin Hoffman's important!
ERNA: Is that what you've learned, that Dustin Hoffman's important? We could have stayed home to find that out.

GREGOR: *(Moves to the bathroom.)* Besides, Erna, why should I bother to read the newspaper when you always read it to me?
ERNA: I don't read it to you—I ask you questions.
GREGOR: If I don't know what's happening—why ask me questions?
ERNA: Good question. Though I think that has something to do with what choices I have.
GREGOR: There are plenty of people who you could talk to.
ERNA: But they don't want to talk to me, Gregor.
GREGOR: Keep telling yourself that and it'll turn out being true.
ERNA: Come shopping with me and you'll find out it already is.
GREGOR: I see now we are back to the subject of my taking you shopping.
ERNA: I didn't know we ever left it. I've just been waiting for you to finish breakfast.
GREGOR: I've finished! There's no food.
ERNA: That's my point about the shopping.
GREGOR: Fine. You want me to take you shopping. I'll take you shopping! Get your purse!
ERNA: Now? You aren't dressed!
GREGOR: *(He goes to the bathroom door.)* Damnit, I'll get dressed! We'll go shopping. We'll come back to this apartment. We'll lock the door. You can continue reading me the newspaper.
ERNA: I don't read you the newspaper.
GREGOR: *(Goes in, and then comes out.)* What the hell, maybe I won't even shave today. After listening to you, you have to ask yourself, what is the god damn point!

(GREGOR closes the door. Pause. Telephone rings.)

ERNA: Telephone, Gregor.
GREGOR: *(Off)* Get it.
ERNA: Gregor!
GREGOR: Erna, pick up the phone!

(She lets it ring.)

GREGOR: Erna! *(He hurries out of the bathroom with shaving cream on his face. Into the phone:)* HELLO? OH, YES. THAT IS VERY NICE. BUT . . . YES, BUT I DO NOT THINK SO. VERY BUSY TONIGHT. SO THANK YOU. YES, I HUG YOU. GOODBYE. *(He hangs up.)*
ERNA: I thought you weren't going to shave.
GREGOR: That was Josef.
ERNA: *(Shrugs.)* He doesn't want to talk to me. *(She takes a cigarette.)*

GREGOR: What makes you think that?

ERNA: I don't think I'm American enough for him.

GREGOR: And I am?

ERNA: You've been trying hard enough, Gregor. *(Pause.)* What did he want?

GREGOR: He invited us to watch the fireworks tonight on the Hudson River.

ERNA: Tonight?

GREGOR: It's American Independence Day.

ERNA: Today?

(She opens her paper.)

GREGOR: That's yesterday's paper. You won't find out anything in there.

ERNA: No. I bought it this morning.

GREGOR: This morning?

ERNA: Yes.

GREGOR: You can go out and buy the paper, but you can't buy food?

ERNA: You can't buy food from a machine, Gregor.

(He moves back toward the bathroom.)

ERNA: You told Josef no?

GREGOR: Of course I told him no.

ERNA: You didn't ask me if I wanted to go.

GREGOR: Because I knew you wouldn't want to go.

ERNA: Who will be there?

(GREGOR shrugs.)

ERNA: I couldn't go.

GREGOR: I didn't ask you to go, Erna.

ERNA: That's just what I was saying.

GREGOR: You want me to call him back and see if we can still go and then I can ask you and you can tell me you don't want to go so I can tell him again we can't go?

(Pause.)

(She looks away. He goes back into the bathroom, then suddenly comes out.)

GREGOR: Just what is it that you want, Erna?!!!

(Pause. He stares at her. She gets up, gets another cigarette, lights it, and goes by him into the bathroom, closing the door. GREGOR takes his toast and butters it. He takes it to the table and sits down to eat, still with shaving cream on his face. ERNA comes out of the bathroom her eyes red from crying. She still smokes. They look at each other.)

ERNA: You don't have any meetings today?
GREGOR: It's a holiday.
(She nods.)
GREGOR: So I can take you shopping.
(She nods, and again takes the newspaper. Pause.)
ERNA: *(Reading)* "THAT IS A LONG HAUL WITH UNCERTAIN RESULTS." Gregor, what does this "LONG HAUL" mean?
GREGOR: "LONG HAUL"? I don't know. Read me the whole sentence, maybe I can figure it out from the context.

SCENE FOUR

Title:
BEFORE

Early evening. ERNA *and* GREGOR *sit on the couch waiting, dressed to go out.*

ERNA: What time is it now?
(He shows her his watch.)
ERNA: Is he late? I haven't learned what's late here.
*(*GREGOR *shrugs. Pause.)*
ERNA: Are you worried about showing the film?
GREGOR: No. *(Pause.)* Just remembering what I went through to make it. That's all. They wouldn't understand here.
ERNA: Other people made it too, Gregor. *(Short pause.)* I made it too. Or don't you remember?
GREGOR: You acted in it.
ERNA: Ah.
GREGOR: You were wonderful, Erna. It'll be nice to see you acting again.
ERNA: Who says I've ever stopped acting?
*(*GREGOR *laughs to himself and nods. Pause.)*
GREGOR: There were things I went through to make this film that even you never imagined.

ERNA: Like what?

GREGOR: Never mind. It's best to forget about all that now.

ERNA: Like what? You mean with the authorities? You think you were the only person to have problems with the authorities? Everyone had problems with the authorities.

GREGOR: Not everyone, Erna. Or have you already forgotten how they do things at home?

ERNA: Who didn't have problems with the authorities, Gregor?

GREGOR: Klima for instance. He never had a problem.

ERNA: Klima's in prison now, Gregor.

GREGOR: I don't mean now, I mean then. When we were all making films. They always approved Klima's scripts. With the rest of us, it was maybe one out of three, but with Klima . . . And that's just how it was with my film, within a week of submitting it, Klima's script was approved. Just like that. Who knew why?

ERNA: So just like that they approved Klima's script —.

GREGOR: They always did, Erna.

ERNA: Then what was the big problem?

(Short pause. He smiles, turns to her, and whispers.)

GREGOR: *(Whispering)* They approved *a* script, Erna, but that's not to say they approved *the* script.

ERNA: You mean there were two scripts for your film?

GREGOR: No, there was only Klima's script. You think I was crazy? But there was also a script in my head, one that hadn't and maybe couldn't be written down.

ERNA: I didn't know that.

GREGOR: No one knew about it — except the cameraman; his family too had been on the list after the war so we understood each other.

ERNA: So there was a big difference between Klima's and your scripts?

GREGOR: A very big difference.

ERNA: And the script I was given on the set — then that was your script.

GREGOR: No, no, that was Klima's.

ERNA: Gregor — but that's the script I learned my lines from.

GREGOR: I know that. Klima was there all the time. I couldn't exactly change his script when he was there.

ERNA: But then you shot Klima's script.

GREGOR: I shot it, yes. But I shot it as if it were my script. I made it very different.

ERNA: Oh.
(She laughs to herself.)

GREGOR: What's funny? It was different, Erna. It wasn't the script Klima had in mind at all.

ERNA: But they were his words.

GREGOR: You can say a lot of different things with the same words! *(Pause.)* Remember the house?

ERNA: The house in the film?

GREGOR: Yes, Erna.

ERNA: Of course I remember it. The big white farm house. The whole film was shot in that house.

GREGOR: I went through hell to shoot my film in that house! I could have shot Klima's script in any old farm house. But not mine. Oh they tried to make me. I spent six months looking for that house. See, I had to have a house just like the one I grew up in. Like the house I was born in. Like the house they took away from us. *(Short pause.)* Nothing else would do.
(Pause.)

ERNA: Gregor, I didn't know—.

GREGOR: In *my* script there had to be this house. *(Short pause.)* I didn't dare just use my family's old house. *(Short pause.)* That would have made them very suspicious. *(Short pause.)* My house. *(He smiles to himself.)* My film. *(Pause.)* See—they won't understand here.

ERNA: *(Taking his hand)* Gregor—.
(Door buzzer.)

GREGOR: That's Josef now.

SCENE FIVE

Title:
AND AFTER

Later that evening. GREGOR *is getting undressed.* ERNA *sits.*

ERNA: We don't belong. I hope that is clear to you now.
GREGOR: Actually I was just thinking the opposite, Erna.
ERNA: Yes?
GREGOR: Yes. *(He gets his pajamas out of a drawer.)* Everyone liked the film, Erna.
ERNA: Everyone wasn't at the cinema, Gregor.
GREGOR: Everyone who was liked it, Erna.
ERNA: You talked to everyone then?
GREGOR: I talked to everyone who talked to me.
ERNA: *(Snickers to herself.)* That's just what I mean.
GREGOR: Erna, they liked it. My film was liked. You can't deny that.
ERNA: And therefore you think they like you.
GREGOR: I didn't say that.
ERNA: If they like your work, they like you. That's how you think.
GREGOR: That is not how I think, Erna.
ERNA: Or is it since they said they liked your film, then you like them.
GREGOR: All I said was they liked it. Damnit Erna, isn't that enough for now?
ERNA: I don't know—is it?
(He ignores her and goes into the bathroom to change.)
ERNA: So maybe they liked it, but that doesn't mean they enjoyed it. I'm not sure they could ever enjoy it like it was meant to be enjoyed.
GREGOR: *(Off)* How was it meant to be enjoyed??!
(Pause.)
ERNA: You know what I mean.
(Pause.)

GREGOR: *(Off)* You talked to people. What did people tell you?
ERNA: I talked to no one.
GREGOR: *(Entering, in his pajamas)* I saw you talking to the manager of the cinema, Erna.
ERNA: Yes, I talked to him.
GREGOR: What did he say about the film?
ERNA: We didn't speak about your film. You think everyone was always speaking about your film? *(Pause.)* We talked about other things.
GREGOR: Good.
ERNA: I asked him how much he paid his workers.

(GREGOR has gone into the kitchen and pours himself a vodka.)

GREGOR: Workers?
ERNA: Yes.

(GREGOR drinks the vodka.)

GREGOR: You asked him how much he paid his workers? What workers, Erna?
ERNA: That's what he asked. I said, the projectionist for example.
GREGOR: And what did the manager of the cinema say?
ERNA: He said the projectionist was a student.

(GREGOR washes the glass in the sink.)

GREGOR: When I was a student, I was a projectionist. Did you know that?
ERNA: We're not talking about you now, Gregor.

(He shrugs, goes to get into bed.)

ERNA: So if the projectionist is a student, then he couldn't be considered a worker. He's an intellectual.
GREGOR: The manager of the cinema said the student was an intellectual?
ERNA: No, he just said he was a student—but isn't that what he meant?
GREGOR: *(In bed now)* I think he meant that he was a student, Erna.

(Pause. She takes another cigarette.)

GREGOR: You know you get headaches when you smoke too much.

(She shrugs.)

GREGOR: Do what you want.
ERNA: That's easy to say.

(Pause. GREGOR sits up.)

GREGOR: They said they liked it. Why would they lie?

ERNA: You're fifty-six years old and you ask why do people lie?

GREGOR: I mean in this case.

ERNA: Maybe it's not that they lied, maybe it's that you didn't understand.

GREGOR: What's not to understand? I don't understand.

ERNA: Maybe they liked it only as a foreign film, Gregor.

GREGOR: But it is a foreign film. I'm foreign. I made it. It's in Czech. There were subtitles.

ERNA: That's what I mean. They liked it because it was foreign. That doesn't mean they enjoyed it, Gregor. *(Pause.)* You don't know Americans, Gregor.

GREGOR: And of course you do.

ERNA: I never claimed that. I never claimed that Americans liked me.

GREGOR: They like you, Erna. Please.

ERNA: Because they like your film, they like you. And because they like you, they like me? Is that what I'm supposed to believe?

(He rolls over, ignoring her.)

ERNA: Gregor? *(Short pause.)* I don't want to lose you.

(Pause. He sits up and looks at her.)

GREGOR: Really? You seem to be trying to.

SCENE SIX

Title:
DUSTIN HOFFMAN

ERNA *stands at the kitchen counter.* GREGOR *sits on the floor opening a large box.*

(Pause. GREGOR *slowly pulls out styrofoam and then a smallish television set.)*

GREGOR: Maybe I should have gotten a color set, what do you think? *(No response.)* It's black and white.
(Pause.)
ERNA: How much did it cost?
GREGOR: The color set? *(She shakes her head.)* There was a sale. We can afford it.
ERNA: Can we?
GREGOR: And Josef said I can take it off my taxes. He said, because I'll use it for business.
ERNA: A television?
GREGOR: Hand me a butter knife.
(She does.)
ERNA: What does it mean—take it off your taxes?
GREGOR: It seems, Erna, that the government will pay for part of the television.
ERNA: The American government buys its people televisions?
GREGOR: That's what Josef says.
ERNA: Does the government make the televisions?
GREGOR: Erna, this is America.
ERNA: How much did we pay and how much did the government pay?
GREGOR: The government hasn't paid anything yet but they will.
ERNA: How much?
GREGOR: I don't know. Ask Josef. *(He screws the antenna on with the knife.)* Look in the newspaper, they say what's on in there.
ERNA: Then how do we know we can afford it, if we don't know how much we pay?

(She hands him the paper.)
ERNA: I went to the consulate today.
(Long pause.)
GREGOR: A television will help you learn English.
ERNA: I said, I went—.
GREGOR: I heard you. *(Short pause.)* Our consulate?
(She nods.)
ERNA: They had the Prague papers. Skreta's opened his *Macbeth*.
GREGOR: I knew that.
ERNA: They say it's spectacular.
GREGOR: Who's they, Erna? The Prague papers? Everything Skreta does they say is spectacular since he went back.
ERNA: There were photographs—it looked spectacular. *(Pause.)* So you bought a television so I would learn English.
GREGOR: I bought it because I wanted it, Erna.
ERNA: You sound like an American already. *(Pause.)* The attaché asked how you were.
GREGOR: He recognized you? Did they follow you? *(She turns away.)* Erna, did they follow you?!
(She turns back, shakes her head.)
GREGOR: How do you know?
ERNA: I went through Macy's department store. I don't think it's possible to follow anyone through Macy's department store.
GREGOR: Erna, please—be careful.
ERNA: I'm the one who always has been careful.
GREGOR: Stop it!
(Pause.)
ERNA: Besides, they know where we live, Gregor. Don't fool yourself.
GREGOR: If they knew where we lived, they would have been harassing us by now. Where's the newspaper with the television programs?
ERNA: It's right there, Gregor.
(He picks it up.)
ERNA: The attaché said we could come back. *(She looks at him and then away.)* Skreta went back.
GREGOR: Skreta had an exit stamp in his passport, Erna. Skreta did not escape through Yugoslavia. Skreta went on an extended holiday. We left. They'll *say* anything, Erna. Don't you know that by now? We can't go back.
(Pause.)

ERNA: The attaché put an exit stamp in my passport.
(She gets up and gets her passport to show him.)
GREGOR: What did you tell them, Erna?
ERNA: There was only the attaché. I only spoke to him.
GREGOR: What did you tell him, Erna?
ERNA: There wasn't anything to say. *(Short pause.)* Gregor, I didn't plan it. I was on the bus and this man looks up at me, he offers me his seat—in Czech. Then he tells me how much he has admired my stage work. He'd seen almost everything, Gregor. I told him he wasn't old enough to have seen everything. He gave me his card—he was the attaché's driver.
GREGOR: His driver on a bus?
(Pause.)
ERNA: He said he understood, Gregor. He didn't pressure me.
GREGOR: But you went to the consulate. *(Short pause.)* Why???!
(She looks at him, takes out a cigarette, lights it, turns away.)
ERNA: You never said how much the television cost.
(Pause.)
GREGOR: Eighty-three dollars. Plus tax.
ERNA: Plus tax? I thought you took it off your tax.
GREGOR: That's a different tax.
(He turns the television on. Flips a channel. ERNA *moves in front of the television.)*
GREGOR: Try a channel.
(She shakes her head. He flips to another channel.)
GREGOR: What are you smirking about?
ERNA: American television.
(She turns away.)
GREGOR: You've seen ten seconds!!
ERNA: I've heard about it.
(She goes back to the kitchen counter. Long pause.)
GREGOR: *(Finally)* Erna, I bought the god damn television so you would learn how to talk to people!!
ERNA: I know how to talk to people. I talked to people today!!
(She puts on her sweater.)
GREGOR: Where are you going now?
ERNA: To buy a newspaper.
(She leaves. Television is on. She returns.)
ERNA: The mail came. There's a letter from Prague.
GREGOR: From your sister?
(She hurries and opens it. GREGOR *has gotten up.)*

ERNA: Here, you read these pages.
  (He takes them. They are devouring the letter. She happens to look up at the television.)
ERNA: Gregor?
GREGOR: *(Over the letter)* What?
ERNA: Isn't that Dustin Hoffman?
GREGOR: *(Looks up at the television.)* Yes.
  (They go back to reading the letter.)

SCENE SEVEN

Title:
THE LAND OF OPPORTUNITY

GREGOR *sits at the table, writing in a small account book.* ERNA *sits with her feet up.*

GREGOR: Ninety-seven dollars in the shoes in the closet. One hundred and thirty-seven taped under the bathroom rug. Four hundred and five dollars in the overhead light.
ERNA: If it hasn't burned up.
GREGOR: It hasn't. *(Pause. He gets up, gets a chair, stands on the chair and checks in the overhead light. Getting down:)* It hasn't. *(He sits back at the table.)* Sixty-five dollars under the mattress. Twelve dollars in the refrigerator.
  (ERNA laughs.)
GREGOR: What's funny?
ERNA: In Prague we hid our friends' plays, here we hide —. *(She laughs.)*
GREGOR: Why is that funny?
ERNA: Not funny, just ironic, that's all.
GREGOR: To you everything is ironic, isn't it?
ERNA: I wish that were true.
  (Pause.)
GREGOR: We still have one thousand, two hundred and fifty-three dollars left of what my cousin loaned us.

ERNA: Loaned *you*. Don't put me in your cousin's debt. He can hardly keep his hands off me as it is.

GREGOR: What an imagination. Everyone either hates you or is trying to paw you. You're not thirty anymore, Erna.

ERNA: I'm sorry?

GREGOR: Forget it.

ERNA: You said I wasn't thirty anymore.

GREGOR: *(Without looking up)* So?

ERNA: Why did you say that?

(He shrugs.)

ERNA: I suppose you are thirty.

GREGOR: I enjoy being the age I am. I'm not ashamed.

ERNA: And I am?

GREGOR: You're an actress, Erna.

ERNA: What is that supposed to mean?

GREGOR: Look, isn't this a stupid thing to argue about?

ERNA: I didn't realize we were arguing.

GREGOR: We were just about to. Trust me.

(Pause. She moves away.)

GREGOR: One thousand, two hundred and fifty-three divided by . . . I think we'll be fine for another four months.

ERNA: Three.

GREGOR: Three and a half.

ERNA: Three.

GREGOR: Three.

ERNA: Maybe two and a half.

GREGOR: Three, Erna.

(Pause.)

ERNA: And then what?

GREGOR: Something will happen. I'm having meetings.

ERNA: Everybody has meetings. I can have meetings.

GREGOR: So have them. *(Short pause.)* They've seen my film. They liked it. They told me they liked it. We have three and a half months.

ERNA: Two.

(Short pause.)

GREGOR: Look, if nothing works out by then, I'll drive a taxi.

ERNA: You'll drive a taxi?

GREGOR: Yes.

ERNA: You don't know how to drive, Gregor.

GREGOR: I'll learn.

ERNA: You'll learn?
GREGOR: That's right.
ERNA: Of course. Why not? When we left you did say in America everything was possible. Unfortunately I did not understand "everything" to mean you learning to drive a car.
GREGOR: It can't be hard. It's something at least.
ERNA: I guess it is. *(Pause.)* I can scrub floors.
GREGOR: You'd do that?
ERNA: Look what I've already done.
GREGOR: "Look what I've already done." I see. New tactic. The martyr. Don't worry, I'm not going to let you scrub floors. *(Short pause.)* I'll scrub floors.
ERNA: But what else can an old former actress do?
GREGOR: Erna, you are not a former actress—
ERNA: But a minute ago you said—
GREGOR: What I said had nothing to do with your acting. I'm sorry I said anything.
(Pause.)
ERNA: Maybe you can get the attaché's chauffeur to teach you how to drive.
(He looks at her.)
ERNA: You could just ask.
(Pause.)
GREGOR: I'm not going to ask for an exit stamp, Erna. We've been through this. I'm on their list. Do you know what that means?
ERNA: But if you said the right things.
GREGOR: I've already said the right things, which is why we left.
ERNA: Which is why you left. *(Pause.)* I left with you. *(Long pause.)* Gregor, it is all coming apart.
GREGOR: Nothing is coming apart.
ERNA: Look up.
(She stands over him. He doesn't look up. He has been looking through a small date book.)
GREGOR: I have three meetings today. *(Pause. Without looking up:)* We have three months.
ERNA: Two and a half. *(She looks away.)*

SCENE EIGHT

Title:
BY THE BOOTSTRAPS

Late evening. GREGOR *is at the open window;* ERNA *is at a distance, watching him. He is drunk.*

GREGOR: *(Shouting out the window)* America, I love you! Do you hear me, America?!
ERNA: I think America's heard enough for one night, Gregor, so you can close the window.
GREGOR: *(Pointing)* America, Erna.
ERNA: Now you tell me. I said close the window. You're drunk.
GREGOR: Yes.
(He moves away from the window. She goes and closes it.)
GREGOR: *(To himself)* Yes. *(He turns to* ERNA.*)* But Erna . . .
ERNA: Yes, Gregor?
GREGOR: I think I have the right to be drunk.
ERNA: That is definitely just one person's opinion.
GREGOR: Besides, the boy producer was paying. *(He laughs to himself.)* He didn't know shit. Erna, did I tell you he has his own theater in this Hartford and he didn't know shit?
ERNA: Is that what you told the producer, Gregor, that he didn't know shit?
GREGOR: What? Erna, don't be stupid. Even in America you can't be stupid.
ERNA: You figured that out by yourself?
GREGOR: I told him I was grateful! I thanked him for considering me. I was charming. And I was grateful. We all should be. You too, Erna.
ERNA: Leave me out of this, please. Have your own fun. I want to go to bed.
GREGOR: Erna . . . ?
ERNA: Now what, Gregor?
GREGOR: I told you about the play, didn't I? I might be directing this play?

ERNA: Tell me again tomorrow. Get undressed. *(Short pause.)* Or maybe you need help?

GREGOR: *(He looks at his clothes, weaves a bit.)* I don't know.

ERNA: *(She goes to undress him.)* Sit down. *(She pushes him down on the couch.)* Pick up your feet. *(He does. She starts to take off his shoes.)*

GREGOR: Erna, we are going to get out of this god damn one room.

ERNA: Not tonight, Gregor. I'm not going anywhere with you tonight.

GREGOR: But I don't mean tonight.

ERNA: No? Lift your arms. *(He does. She pulls the sweater over his head.)*

GREGOR: Three months. We had only three months. This boy was really impressed with me. As well he should be.

ERNA: Impressed with how much you could drink?

GREGOR: Erna, it's about time we got something, do you understand?

ERNA: What something would you like to get? Another television set?

GREGOR: *(Getting up)* Erna—

ERNA: Stay still.

GREGOR: *(Moving toward the window)* I want you to look at this with me . . .

ERNA: Gregor, leave that window closed. *(He does.)* And please keep your voice down.

GREGOR: *(He nods and begins to whisper.)* Look at all that. That is here, Erna. We are here. I mean . . .
(Short pause.)

ERNA: What do you mean?
(Pause. He looks out the window.)

ERNA: Sit down and I'll take your pants off.

GREGOR: *(Still at the window)* Listen to me! Sh-sh. This is the world today. Like it or not, Erna, understand? *(She sits down.)* This is . . . culture. Call it shit, Erna. Go ahead. But that's fine. Shit is fine. And we found it. It is ours. We're here.
(He goes and sits next to her. He lifts his legs.)

GREGOR: Take my pants off. *(She begins to.)* I just want to see your attaché friend's face when he hears. I was choked, but I didn't strangle.

ERNA: He's not my friend, Gregor. And besides I doubt if he'll even hear.
GREGOR: Oh they hear. They're probably in the next room hearing right now.
ERNA: Gregor.
GREGOR: Figuratively. Figuratively, Erna.
ERNA: I'll get your pajamas. *(She goes toward the bathroom.)*
GREGOR: Wait! *(He jumps up with his pants around his ankles.)* I want you to understand one thing. One thing you are not understanding, Erna.
ERNA: What is that?
GREGOR: Understand that if a man can achieve something in this world, Erna. Here! In America. Then—
ERNA: Then what?
GREGOR: Then, he achieves everywhere. Just by achieving here. That's what this is. It's the center.
ERNA: I don't understand.
GREGOR: Wait! If a man's a poet here, Erna. Listen to me!!! He is not a Czech poet here, Erna. He is a poet. Period. That's what I mean. That's what this is all about. That's why everyone wants to be here.
(Short pause.)
ERNA: Not everyone, Gregor.
GREGOR: Who?! Who?! No one we know, Erna.
(Pause.)
ERNA: Here, put your own pajamas on. *(She throws him his pajamas.)*
GREGOR: I can. I can.
(He tries. She picks up a blanket and moves toward the bathroom.)
GREGOR: What are you doing?
ERNA: I'm going to sleep in the bathroom.
GREGOR: Oh.
(She goes into the bathroom, closes the door. He tries to put his pajamas on and falls. She comes out and looks at him.)
GREGOR: I can do it myself!!!
(She goes back into the bathroom and slams the door.)

SCENE NINE

Title:
SHADOWS

Evening. GREGOR *is at the table, looking through a photo album. Bread on the table.* ERNA *lights candles.*

ERNA: Where is this Hartford?
GREGOR: *(Without looking up)* In the north. I could take a train. Why didn't you tell me before that you'd brought these photographs?
ERNA: I didn't? *(He looks up.)* I must have been waiting for the right time.
(He smiles, looks back down.)
ERNA: Here's a knife to cut the bread with. *(Gives him the knife.)*
GREGOR: *(Looking at a photo)* Vlasta in my *Lower Depths*. I haven't thought about Vlasta for years.
ERNA: Vlasta's been dead for years, Gregor.
GREGOR: For years?
(She nods. He shakes his head. Pause.)
ERNA: The food last night with the producer, was it good?
GREGOR: The food?
ERNA: In the restaurant.
GREGOR: Yes, it was very good.
ERNA: Oh. *(Short pause.)* Perhaps you're not very hungry then.
GREGOR: *(Without looking up)* I'm hungry.
ERNA: Maybe you ate too much last night.
GREGOR: No, I'm— *(He looks at her.)* I'm hungry, Erna.
ERNA: Good.
*(*GREGOR *looks back over the album.)*
GREGOR: Lukash, Erna.
ERNA: Lukash?
(She goes to him.)
ERNA: Where? *(He points.)* That's Lukash? In *The Lower Depths?* He wasn't in *The Lower Depths*.

GREGOR: This isn't *The Lower Depths*. I can't figure out what this is. It isn't one of mine. But that's Lukash.
ERNA: Yes. That's Lukash. I don't think I saw this play. *(Moves to go back to the kitchen.)*
GREGOR: Wait. I remember. It's another Gorky. The one they closed.
ERNA: They closed a Gorky?
GREGOR: In rehearsal they closed it. They're in rehearsal clothes, see? Erna, where did you get these photographs?
ERNA: From friends, Gregor.
(She goes and gets a bottle of wine.)
GREGOR: *(Being shown the bottle)* What is this?
ERNA: Will you open it?
GREGOR: Czech wine? Erna, where did you find Czech wine?
ERNA: In the store. Just open it, please.
GREGOR: You asked for Czech wine?
ERNA: Why not?
(She goes and gets a cigarette; GREGOR smiles to himself and shakes his head. He looks back at the album as ERNA holds up a large book.)
ERNA: Gregor. . . ?
GREGOR: *(Looking up)* What is it?
ERNA: I borrowed it from the library.
GREGOR: You went to the library? When?
ERNA: *(Reading the title)* "Photographs of Prague." I thought you might . . .
GREGOR: *(Smiling)* Yes.
(She sets the book back down.)
GREGOR: Thank you. Why don't you sit down.
ERNA: In a minute. I want to put in the pie.
(She goes to the oven.)
GREGOR: You're making a pie? *(Short pause.)* Erna, I think you're trying to seduce me.
ERNA: Think whatever you want. I'm making a pie.
(Pause. She puts the pie into the oven.)
GREGOR: *(Looking over the album)* Erna, your *Three Sisters*.
ERNA: My Olga? *(Goes to him.)*
GREGOR: No. Your Irina, I think.
ERNA: Yes. That's my Irina. Gregor, these are old.
GREGOR: Very old.
ERNA: Not that old. *(She moves back to the oven.)*
GREGOR: Pavek as Sganarelle.

ERNA: Pavek? Really? *(She wipes her hands and goes to see.)*
GREGOR: Why are you so interested in Pavek?
ERNA: I liked Pavek.
GREGOR: I didn't know that.
ERNA: You knew I liked Pavek.
GREGOR: No. I didn't know. When did you like him?
ERNA: Gregor, I only liked him. He was a great actor.
GREGOR: I see.
ERNA: Gregor — Pavek was a homosexual. We were friends.
GREGOR: Pavek? You know you shouldn't say that.
ERNA: Gregor, I can say it here.
GREGOR: I suppose so. *(Short pause.)* Pavek a homosexual? I didn't know.
ERNA: That's why he killed himself.
GREGOR: I thought he killed himself because of gambling. That's what we all thought.
ERNA: I know that's what everyone thought. But he didn't gamble, Gregor. He was caught. He didn't want his daughter to know. He killed himself.
GREGOR: You knew this?
ERNA: We talked. If he killed himself there wouldn't be a trial. And his son-in-law could keep his job as a foreman. They made it all very clear to him.
GREGOR: He told you all this?
ERNA: Yes.
GREGOR: What did you say to him?
ERNA: What could I say?
GREGOR: Then you knew he was going to kill himself?
ERNA: I knew he was thinking about it. I told him to emigrate.
GREGOR: He wouldn't do that.
ERNA: No.
GREGOR: Not with his son-in-law being a foreman. He'd never be able to live with himself. He was too sensitive.
ERNA: He was very sensitive. *(Looks at the album.)* That's not Pavek.
GREGOR: That's Marek as Don Juan. See that shadow —
ERNA: Yes.
GREGOR: That's Pavek.
ERNA: The shadow?
GREGOR: Can't you tell?
ERNA: Yes. That's Pavek. Of course.

GREGOR: He was a lovely man. Beautiful.
ERNA: His daughter was lovely too.
GREGOR: He lived for her. How was he caught?
ERNA: In the train station.
GREGOR: I didn't know that. They kept it all very quiet. Usually something like that everyone knows.
ERNA: Everyone didn't know. That's why he had to shoot himself.
(Pause. GREGOR looks at more photos.)
GREGOR: I can't figure out where you got all these. Half of them I've never seen before.
ERNA: *(Going back into the kitchen)* I had them.
GREGOR: With you? At home?
ERNA: I collected them from our friends.
GREGOR: Oh.
ERNA: Before we left.
GREGOR: Oh. Well it's nice to have something to remember Prague by.
ERNA: We have many things to remember Prague by, Gregor.
(Pause. GREGOR laughs.)
ERNA: What?
GREGOR: Bruz in the Feydeau.
(Without looking at the picture, she laughs too. He turns to another page.)
ERNA: So you will be gone how long?
GREGOR: Five weeks. If I go.
ERNA: If? I thought—
GREGOR: I haven't been given a contract yet.
ERNA: Huh.
GREGOR: What does that mean?
ERNA: It means—huh.
(Pause.)
GREGOR: *(Over the album)* Look at Vanek's set for *The Cherry Orchard*, Erna.
(She goes and looks and then moves back to the kitchen.)
ERNA: We could write Vanek. He's in Paris, isn't he?
GREGOR: No.
ERNA: He's not in Paris?
GREGOR: You know as well as I know that Vanek went back, Erna.
ERNA: I forgot.

GREGOR: *(Without looking at her)* No you didn't.
(Pause.)
ERNA: And in this Hartford, they have good sets?
GREGOR: I don't know.
ERNA: But you said you saw pictures.
GREGOR: I saw plans. For the stage. I didn't see pictures.
ERNA: They didn't show you pictures?
GREGOR: No. *(Short pause.)* It's a highly regarded theater, Erna.
(Pause.)
ERNA: I just don't know how they put on plays in America in just five weeks.
GREGOR: I'd rather not talk about it. I don't want to get my hopes up.
ERNA: No. You don't.
GREGOR: Even if I don't get the job, we should at least be pleased that people are beginning to think of me.
ERNA: A lot of people think of you, Gregor. *(Pause. She goes back to the kitchen. Then, noticing the expression on his face:)* What's wrong?
GREGOR: *(Holding some loose photos)* What is this?
ERNA: What?
GREGOR: These pictures.
ERNA: *(Over his shoulder)* I don't know.
GREGOR: Who gave these to you?
ERNA: Those? I don't remember.
GREGOR: Did Marek give them to you?
ERNA: Most of our friends gave me pictures, Gregor. What are they of?
GREGOR: Marek's party he gave for me.
ERNA: I wasn't there.
GREGOR: I know you weren't there. I remember everyone who was there. There were five of us. And no one was taking pictures. No one would at a party like that.
ERNA: Obviously someone took pictures. There they are.
GREGOR: This is a joke.
ERNA: What is?
GREGOR: Erna, what I said at that party is what I was denounced for.
ERNA: Gregor—!
GREGOR: What I said to the officials later didn't help. But what I said at that party was the start.

ERNA: They are dark. Gregor, I didn't know.
GREGOR: This is someone's idea of a joke.
ERNA: It's a sick joke, Gregor.
GREGOR: When you asked our friends for pictures, did you say why?
ERNA: No. But I'm sure they knew.
GREGOR: Yes.
ERNA: They could see it in our faces.
GREGOR: Yes.
ERNA: We could always see it in someone's face before he left. *(Pause. She sits.)* Marek gave me some. Also Bruz. Jaroslav—.
GREGOR: Jaroslav. I never did trust Jaroslav.
ERNA: He denounced you?
GREGOR: I don't know. *(Short pause.)* I don't know. *(Short pause.)* In any case, it doesn't matter now.
ERNA: No?
(Pause.)
GREGOR: Blow out the candles. I want to turn on some lights, it's dark in here.
(She blows out the candles.)

SCENE TEN

Title:
THE FREE WORLD

GREGOR *sits.* ERNA *is in the kitchen. She takes a kettle, fills it with water, places it on the stove.*

GREGOR: So you won't go?
(She shrugs.)
GREGOR: It's ten to twelve. The producer said he'd see you at twelve.
ERNA: I never said I would, Gregor.
GREGOR: But I thought . . .
ERNA: Then maybe you thought wrong.

GREGOR: Yes. I'll call him later and apologize for you not showing up.
ERNA: I don't want you apologizing for me.
GREGOR: You don't leave me any choice, Erna.
ERNA: So now I'm hurting you.
GREGOR: You're not hurting me. I don't care what you do.
ERNA: Is that true?
GREGOR: It's a free world here, do what you want.
ERNA: You don't want that, Gregor.
GREGOR: I wouldn't bet on that.
(Pause. They look at each other.)
GREGOR: It wasn't much of a part. And who knows if you'd even have gotten it. It was only an audition.
ERNA: I'd have gotten it.
GREGOR: How do you know? You don't know how things are done here.
ERNA: I know because my husband is directing the play.
GREGOR: Erna, is that why—?
ERNA: I don't know! *(Short pause.)* Please, just leave me alone for now.
(He nods and stands up.)
ERNA: Where are you going?
GREGOR: You just said you wanted me to leave you alone.
ERNA: That doesn't mean I don't want to know where you're going.
GREGOR: I'm going to take a shower. *(He moves to the bathroom.)* Josef's coming by. Let him in when he buzzes.
ERNA: Josef's coming by?
GREGOR: I asked him over when I thought you'd be out.
ERNA: Josef can come when I'm here.
GREGOR: He doesn't speak Czech, Erna. You'd have to speak English. I didn't know if you were ready for that.
(He goes into the bathroom.)
ERNA: Gregor—!
(He closes the door. After a moment we hear the shower turned on. ERNA *throws herself on the couch, after turning on the television. Pause. Suddenly she sits up, looks at her watch, gets up, and puts her coat on. She calls:)*
ERNA: Gregor, will you call the producer and tell him I'll be late?!!
GREGOR: *(Off)* I can't hear you, Erna!

ERNA: I said, call the—
(Buzzer sounds.)
ERNA: Gregor, I think it's—
GREGOR: *(Off)* Is that Josef?
ERNA: Gregor?!
GREGOR: *(Off)* Push the button, Erna! He's downstairs!
(She picks up the buzzer/phone.)
ERNA: HELLO? HELLO? *(She pushes buttons.)* Gregor, no one is—
(The water boils, the kettle whistles. Into the phone:)
ERNA: JUST A—
(The telephone rings. In a bit of a panic:)
ERNA: Gregor!!
(Phone rings.)
GREGOR: *(Off)* Answer the phone!!
(She hurries to the phone; the kettle is whistling, television is on. On her way she knocks over a glass.)
ERNA: *(Into phone)* HELLO? I AM SORRY?
GREGOR: *(Off)* Was that Josef?
ERNA: *(Into phone)* WHAT? I DO NOT—
(Knock at the door.)
ERNA: Just a minute. ONE MOMENT PLEASE. *(Into phone)* Can you speak to my husband? I AM SORRY, I WAS SPEAKING CZECH. I SAID, CAN YOU—
GREGOR: *(Off)* What are you doing out there?! Let him in, Erna!
ERNA: *(Into phone)* HELLO? I DO NOT UNDERSTAND, MISTER—
(Another knock; she calls back:)
ERNA: I DO COME! *(Into phone)* IF I BUY MAGAZINES I WIN FREE TRIP TO THIS MIAMI BEACH????
(Television, whistling kettle, knocking. GREGOR *comes out in his robe.)*
GREGOR: *(Yells.)* Erna!!!
ERNA: *(Pleading)* Gregor!

SCENE ELEVEN

Title:

GOING PLACES

ERNA *sits at the table. In front of her is an English grammar book. As she practices she covers with one hand the line she is supposed to figure out.*

ERNA: I WILL GO TO THE PARK.
I GO TO THE PARK.
I HAVE . . . GONE TO THE PARK.
I . . . *(Checks.)* WENT? What is this WENT? *(Short pause.)*
HE WILL GO TO THE SCHOOL.
HE GOES TO THE SCHOOL.
HE HAS GONE TO THE SCHOOL.
HE WENT TO THE SCHOOL. *(Short pause.)*
SHE . . . WILL GO TO THE REFRIGERATOR.
(She gets up and moves to the refrigerator.)
SHE GOES TO THE REFRIGERATOR.
(She opens the refrigerator door, looks, closes it without finding anything she wants.)
SHE HAS GONE TO THE REFRIGERATOR.
(She sits back at the table.)
SHE WENT TO THE REFRIGERATOR.
(Continues with the book:)
YOU WILL GO TO THE POST OFFICE.
YOU GO TO THE POST OFFICE.
YOU HAVE GONE TO THE POST OFFICE.
YOU WENT TO THE POST OFFICE. *(Short pause.)*
WE WILL GO TO THE CITY.
WE GO TO THE CITY.
WE HAVE GONE. . . . *(She stops. Pause.)*
(Quietly, looking up) WE WILL GO . . . HOME.
WE GO . . . HOME.
WE HAVE GONE . . . HOME.
WE WENT . . . HOME. *(Pause.)*

SCENE TWELVE

Title:
SIBERIA

ERNA *is ironing.* GREGOR *sits, writing down something on a small piece of paper. He has a pile of books in front of him.*

(Pause. He gets up.)
GREGOR: Here's the phone numbers for the theater and my hotel.
(He holds it out. She nods, but doesn't look at him or take the paper.)
GREGOR: I'll set it on the table. *(She nods.)*
(Pause.)
GREGOR: You are going to be all right, aren't you?
ERNA: Of course. Why wouldn't I be all right? What time was your train?
GREGOR: I have an hour.
(He goes back to sorting through the books, trying to decide what to take.)
ERNA: If you end up needing one of those, I can mail it to you.
GREGOR: Thank you. *(Short pause.)* You're going to wear that shirt out if you keep ironing it.
ERNA: *(Shrugs.)* I want you to look nice . . . I think Americans judge you by how you look.
GREGOR: Since when, Erna?
ERNA: It's not true?
GREGOR: If you'd seen the producer of the theater—I doubt if he's worn an ironed shirt all his adult life.
ERNA: But he's still a boy. The boys can dress like that. You're not a boy anymore, Gregor.
GREGOR: If you're only worried about how I *look*, then why have you been up since five pressing my underwear?
(Short pause.)
ERNA: I just wanted to.
(He smiles. She finishes ironing, folds the shirt, and puts it in the suitcase. He writes something.)
GREGOR: Here, you'll need the address of the theater if you're go-

ing to send anything. *(She doesn't look at him.)* I'll put it with the phone numbers. *(He does. Pause.)* I asked Josef to look in on you. *(She nods.)* Maybe the two of you can go to a show. *(Pause.)*

ERNA: Maybe.
(Pause.)

GREGOR: After all, it's only five weeks, Erna. And then you'll come to Hartford for the opening.

ERNA: I'll never understand how Americans can rehearse their plays in only five weeks.
(Pause.)

GREGOR: You will come up for the opening, won't you?

ERNA: I might be going to a show that night with Josef.
(He smiles. He packs some books in a bag. Long pause. She closes the suitcase.)

ERNA: There's instant coffee in the bag. And I made you a lunch—cheese and salami. It's in the refrigerator. I'll get it. *(She does.)* And there's toilet paper—

GREGOR: I think the hotel will have toilet paper.

ERNA: *(Ignoring him)* And I packed the clock—

GREGOR: What will you use?

ERNA: You can figure out the time by watching the television. There's two bars of soap with the toilet paper, and your coat brush.

GREGOR: I'll be sure to brush off the blond hairs before I come home.
(ERNA looks up at him, then smiles.)

ERNA: And two cartons of cigarettes. The matches I stuffed in your slippers—

GREGOR: Erna, I'm not going to Siberia.
(Long pause.)

ERNA: Help me put the ironing board away.
(He does. They set it in the kitchen area. He takes her hand. She tries not to cry.)

GREGOR: Erna . . .
(He hugs her, she hugs back. Pause. Then lights fade.)

SCENE THIRTEEN

Title:
HIS MEMORY

This scene is GREGOR's *memory of their first moments in the apartment. Stage empty. Door opens,* GREGOR *then* ERNA *enter with suitcases.*

GREGOR: HELLO? IS SOMEONE IN HERE PLEASE? *(To* ERNA*)* No one's here.
(They look around.)
ERNA: *(Pointing to the door buzzer)* What is this?
GREGOR: To let people in the front door. *(Noticing something on the table)* She left a note. *(He reads.)* "DEAR MR. AND MRS. HASEK. SORRY I COULDN'T WELCOME YOU MYSELF, BUT BUSINESS IN L.A. CALLS."
ERNA: What is "L.A."?
GREGOR: Los Angeles. *(Continues to read.)* "ENJOY THE SUBLET. FEEL FREE TO USE ANYTHING HERE. AND IF YOU HAVE ANY QUESTIONS JUST CALL THE SUPER."
ERNA: What is this "SUPER"?
GREGOR: It's nice, don't you think?
ERNA: Is that the bedroom?
GREGOR: *(Opens a door.)* A closet. I don't think there is a bedroom. The couch folds out.
ERNA: I see. *(She opens her bag for a cigarette, then notices.)* Gregor — the refrigerator!
GREGOR: My God.
ERNA: Why is it so big?
GREGOR: I don't know. *(He opens it.)* Erna, she left a bottle of vodka for us.
ERNA: It's not for us, Gregor.
GREGOR: Of course it's for us. Look in the cabinets for some glasses.
ERNA: I don't think we should, Gregor.
GREGOR: There are a couple here in the sink.

(He opens the vodka.)
ERNA: Gregor, it's not ours.
(He hands her a glass.)
GREGOR: *(Toasts.)* To our new home.

SCENE FOURTEEN

Title:
HER MEMORY

This scene is ERNA's *memory of their first moments in the apartment. As in the previous scene,* ERNA *and* GREGOR *with suitcases;* GREGOR *has found the note.*

GREGOR: (Reading) "DEAR MR. AND MRS. HASEK. SORRY I COULDN'T WELCOME YOU MYSELF, BUT BUSINESS IN L.A. CALLS. *(To* ERNA*)* What is 'L.A.'? *(She shrugs.) (Reading)* "I'M SURE YOU WILL TREAT MY HOME AS IF IT WERE YOURS. ANY PROBLEMS JUST CALL THE SUPER."
ERNA: Call what?
GREGOR: *(Shrugs.)* I don't know.
ERNA: *(Pointing to the buzzer)* What is this?
GREGOR: *(Shrugs.)* To call the concierge? I don't think there's a bedroom.
ERNA: Maybe the couch folds out. Gregor—the refrigerator!
GREGOR: What do you need a refrigerator that big for?
(They look at each other. GREGOR *opens the refrigerator.)*
GREGOR: There's some vodka. *(Short pause.)* Do you think we should . . . ?
ERNA: I don't know, Gregor?
GREGOR: She left it in the refrigerator.
ERNA: I wouldn't.
GREGOR: Maybe just a little, she'll never know.
(He takes two glasses out of the sink. Pause.)
ERNA: What's wrong?

GREGOR: I'm just tired.
ERNA: Come here.
(She takes him by the hand.)
GREGOR: *(Scared.)* Well, we made it. To us??
   (She nods. They drink.)
GREGOR: Don't you want to take off your coat?
ERNA: I'm not ready yet. Everything's still too new.
GREGOR: It's nice, isn't it? *(She holds him around the waist.)* Isn't it?
   (He looks out the window.) Erna . . . ?
ERNA: What?
GREGOR: Look at those buildings. They're very tall, aren't they?
ERNA: *(Nods.)* Gregor, let's try not to be scared.
   (Pause.)
GREGOR: We will try again here.
ERNA: We have each other, Gregor.
   (They hug.)

SCENE FIFTEEN

Title:
SIBERIA CONTINUED

The same as at the end of Scene Twelve. They are hugging. ERNA *slips something into* GREGOR's *hand.*

GREGOR: What's this?
ERNA: Don't look at it now.
   (She moves away to get his coat.)
GREGOR: A picture? Of you?
ERNA: Look at it on the train.
   (She helps him put on his coat.)
GREGOR: Thank you. *(Short pause.)* Erna, what's left in the refrigerator for you?
ERNA: Plenty. Don't worry.
   (He nods. He picks up his bags.)

GREGOR: I'll call when I get there. *(She nods.)* You take care. Please.

(She nods. He hesitates.)

ERNA: You're going to miss your train.

(He kisses her on the cheek.)

ERNA: Will you go, I want to wash the dishes.

(He smiles. Nods. And slowly leaves. She closes the door behind him. She sighs, almost shaking now. She goes into the kitchen, turns the water on, then suddenly hurries to the window, leaving the water running. She watches out the window and then sees him.)

ERNA: Look up. Look up! Look —

(She waves — he has looked up. She smiles, watches him walk down the street, turns back to the room, sits. She takes out a cigarette. She gets up and locks the chain lock on the door. She goes back and sits. The water runs.)

SCENE SIXTEEN

Title:

A FEW DAYS BEFORE

Rain on the window. GREGOR, *on the couch, in his robe, a thermometer in his mouth.* ERNA *is in the kitchen taking groceries out of a bag. She has just come in and still wears her coat.*

(Pause. Then GREGOR *takes out the thermometer and looks at it, then he shakes it.* ERNA *watches this. He senses this and turns to her.)*

GREGOR: I'm fine. *(Short pause.)* I'll soon be fine.

(Pause.)

ERNA: *(While unpacking)* I'll go to the pharmacy; what you need is a little camphor oil.

GREGOR: You just came back. It's raining.

ERNA: If you're going to Hartford you can't be sick.

GREGOR: "If"?

(Short pause.)

ERNA: When. When. I'll put hot water on for tea and then I'll go.

GREGOR: Erna. . . .

ERNA: *(Takes a newspaper out of the bag.)* Here's the paper if you want it. *(She goes to the couch to hand it to him.)*

GREGOR: Erna. *(He grabs her.)*

ERNA: I'll just be gone a minute, Gregor. I'm not deserting you. *(Notices his expression.)* What?

(He reaches under a cushion and takes out a large envelope.)

GREGOR: *(As he takes out a newspaper clipping and a letter)* This came. From my cousin. Skreta wrote him and offered me two productions for the season. This was enclosed.

(Shows her the newspaper clipping.)

GREGOR: The party paper. It's a summary of my career in the party paper. *(Reads.)* "Gregor Hasek, Director of extraordinary vision." *(Short pause.)* They praise me. I leave the country and they praise me.

(ERNA takes the paper and begins to read.)

GREGOR: At the end of the article they say I've been sick for the past months. I'm resting by the Black Sea.

ERNA: You're by the Black Sea?

GREGOR: That's what they say. *(Short pause.)* I've been sick.

(Short pause, then suddenly they both laugh, and shake their heads. ERNA continues to read, sitting now on the couch. GREGOR gets up and goes into the kitchen. As he makes himself an instant coffee he watches ERNA as she reads.)

GREGOR: *(Finally)* Skreta could protect me.

ERNA: No one can protect you.

GREGOR: No.

(Pause.)

ERNA: *(Turns to look at him.)* But if anyone could, it would be Skreta.

GREGOR: True.

ERNA: *(More to herself)* Two productions.

GREGOR: *(As he stirs his coffee)* Do you think we should go back?

ERNA: *(Excited, she stands and goes to get a cigarette from her purse.)* I try not to think anymore.

(She goes back to the couch. Pause. Neither looks at the other.)

GREGOR: Maybe we should.

ERNA: You don't want that. You have your career in Hartford to think about now. *(She turns to him; he is holding his face and shaking.)* Why are you shaking?

GREGOR: I'm sick. I'm by the Black Sea. *(Short pause.)* Wouldn't it make you happy?

ERNA: To be by the Black Sea? I never liked the Black Sea, Gregor. *(He turns and stares at her.)* I wouldn't mind the mountains, Gregor.

GREGOR: Just tell me what is right. I want to know what will make you happy.

ERNA: Are those now the same question?

GREGOR: Erna—

ERNA: Are those now the same question, Gregor?!!

GREGOR: I want what you want!

ERNA: That's not true! That's never been true! *(Beat.)* Sometimes it's been true.

GREGOR: I want you to get better!

ERNA: I'm not the one who's sick. I'm not the one who is sick, you understand that, don't you?!

GREGOR: *(Pointing to the newspaper clipping)* To tell you the truth I thought you'd be overjoyed.

ERNA: You won't go.

GREGOR: I would for you.

ERNA: I don't want you to go for me.

GREGOR: Can't I do something for you?! Can you only do things for me?!!!

(Long pause.)

ERNA: *(Quietly)* Then let's go home.

GREGOR: Fine.

ERNA: When?

GREGOR: Whenever. *(Nods to her.)*

(ERNA suddenly gets up and goes to the closet.)

GREGOR: What are you doing?

ERNA: I'm packing.

GREGOR: So it really is what you want.

ERNA: It is.

GREGOR: We just leave?

ERNA: That's right.

GREGOR: You really want me to do that.

ERNA: Yes, I do.

GREGOR: *(Yells.)* You would do that to me?!!

ERNA: Gregor??

GREGOR: I thought you loved me. *(He shakes his head, moves toward the bathroom, then suddenly turns back.)* Did you hear what I said?!! I thought you loved me!!

(He goes into the bathroom, slamming the door.)

ERNA: Gregor??

SCENE SEVENTEEN

Title:
ERNA RECALLS AN EARLIER SCENE

Morning, weeks earlier. ERNA *stands by the window with an English-language copy of Chekhov's* Three Sisters *in her hand.* GREGOR, *in his robe, sits on the couch; he smokes, drinks coffee. In front of him is another copy of* Three Sisters, *which he is following.*

(Pause.)

GREGOR: *(Lighting a cigarette)* Whenever you're ready.

(She nods.)

ERNA: *(Reads:)* "ONE YEAR AGO ON THIS VERY DAY, MAY FIFTH—"

GREGOR: *(Correcting her pronunciation, as he does throughout the scene)* FIFTH. MAY FIFTH, Erna.

ERNA: "MAY FIFTH—ON YOUR BIRTHDAY, IRINA—FATHER DIED. IT WAS BITTER COLD AND SNOWING."

GREGOR: COLD. AND. I'm not hearing the D's.

ERNA: COLD. AND. "AT THE TIME, IT ALL SEEMED MORE THAN I COULD BEAR; YOU FAINTED, I EVEN THOUGHT YOU HAD DIED."

GREGOR: "I EVEN THOUGHT YOU HAD DIED."

ERNA: "I EVEN THOUGHT YOU HAD DIED."

GREGOR: It's one phrase. "I EVEN THOUGHT YOU HAD DIED."

ERNA: "I EVEN THOUGHT YOU HAD DIED." *(Continues.)* "IT'S BEEN ONLY A YEAR, WE CAN BARELY REMEMBER IT. YOU'RE BACK WEARING WHITE; YOUR FACE GLOWS."

GREGOR: It's—"WEARING WHITE."
ERNA: " . . . WEARING WHITE; YOUR FACE GLOWS."
GREGOR: *(Taking a sip of coffee)* Bong. Bong. Bong.
ERNA: "THE CLOCK STRUCK THEN TOO."
GREGOR: You should turn to the clock. See the clock.
ERNA: See the clock?
GREGOR: Yes.
ERNA: I should turn and see the clock here?
GREGOR: Yes.
ERNA: I never turn to see the clock here. Two hundred performances of *Three Sisters* and I have never turned here. Olga doesn't move here.
GREGOR: It's better if she turns. In my production she turned.
ERNA: In our production she didn't, Gregor. Skreta didn't want me to turn. You must have seen that production twenty times, why didn't you ever say anything before?
GREGOR: Skreta was the director, Erna. Just try it, you'll see.
ERNA: I'll see what?
GREGOR: That I'm right.
ERNA: So I should turn here.
GREGOR: Yes.
ERNA: Why?
GREGOR: Why? . . . I don't remember why, Erna. My production was ten years ago. I just remember it worked. And that's what we're after.
ERNA: That it works? That's not what we're after, Gregor.
GREGOR: Will you just try it?
(Pause.)
ERNA: *(Reading)* "IT'S BEEN ONLY A YEAR, WE CAN BARELY REMEMBER IT. YOU'RE BACK WEARING WHITE—"
GREGOR: "WHITE," Erna.
ERNA: "WHITE; YOUR FACE GLOWS."
GREGOR: *(As the clock)* Bong. Bong. Bong.
ERNA: *(Turns.)* "THE CLOCK STRUCK THEN TOO." *(Short pause.)* I turned.
GREGOR: And?
ERNA: And I don't like it. I shouldn't turn there. I never did.
GREGOR: Fine, then just forget it. Forget I said anything! Forget I'm even here! What do I care, it's your audition.
ERNA: It's not my audition, Gregor. I never said I was going to

audition. I said I wanted to practice in case I started to think like I might go to the audition, Gregor.
GREGOR: Whatever you say. Though I seem to recall that it was you who asked me to help.
ERNA: To help with my English. I don't need direction. I had a director. Skreta directed me.
GREGOR: And Skreta's a fine director.
(Short pause.)
ERNA: So I'm not turning here?
GREGOR: Ask Skreta.
(Short pause.)
ERNA: *(Continues.)* "I REMEMBER THEM CARRYING FATHER AWAY."
GREGOR: *(A little hostile now)* "FATHER!" With a "TH"!
ERNA: "I REMEMBER THEM CARRYING FATHER AWAY." In the Czech it's different. In the Czech it's "taking Father out of our house."
GREGOR: Then say that.
ERNA: But it says in the English—
GREGOR: Say what you want to say, Erna.
ERNA: I want to say what Chekhov wanted.
GREGOR: I don't think Chekhov's going to be at the audition, Erna. But if he is, we'll ask him what he likes.
(She looks at him. Pause.)
ERNA: "I REMEMBER THEM CARRYING FATHER AWAY. THE BAND . . ." *(To GREGOR)* BAND???
GREGOR: You know what it means.
(She mimes a horn player.)
GREGOR: Keep going.
ERNA: "THE BAND PLAYED A MARCH, THEY FIRED RIFLE SHOTS OVER THE GRAVE. FOR A GENERAL OF THE BRIGADE THERE WEREN'T MANY MOURNERS . . ." Correct me whenever you want, Gregor.
(He says nothing.)
ERNA: ". . . THERE WEREN'T MANY MOURNERS. WELL, IT WAS RAINING HARD, RAIN MIXED WITH SNOW." Here I turn my head.
(She does; GREGOR snickers.)
ERNA: What's funny about that?
GREGOR: Don't ask me, I'm not the director.

(Pause.)
ERNA: Here Irina says—
GREGOR: *(Reads.)* "WHY THINK ABOUT IT?"
ERNA: That's all?
GREGOR: That's all.
ERNA: In the Czech it's much longer. *(Shakes her head.)* Language. *(Continues reading.)* "NOW TODAY IT'S WARM. WE CAN EVEN KEEP THE WINDOWS OPEN. THOUGH THERE STILL AREN'T ANY LEAVES ON THE BIRCHES . . . " *(She gets a small smile on her face and looks out the window.)* This is true, no leaves on any birches out there. *(*GREGOR *just looks at her.)*
ERNA: *(Continues.)* "ON THE BIRCHES. IT'S BEEN ELEVEN YEARS SINCE FATHER WAS PUT IN CHARGE OF THE BRIGADE."
GREGOR: *(Without looking up)* "BRIGADE."
ERNA: "BRIGADE AND WE ALL HAD TO LEAVE MOSCOW."
GREGOR: "AND WE ALL HAD TO LEAVE MOSCOW." It's all one sentence.
ERNA: "AND WE ALL HAD TO LEAVE MOSCOW. I REMEMBER WELL, THAT AT THIS TIME, IN EARLY MAY, THE SUN BATHES EVERYTHING."
GREGOR: It's BATHES, Erna. BATHES.
ERNA: BATHES.
GREGOR: BATHES. BATHES! God damnit!!
ERNA: What's wrong with you?
(He gets up with the book and moves away.)
ERNA: *(Continues.)* "AFTER ELEVEN YEARS, I REMEMBER IT ALL AS IF IT WERE YESTERDAY."
GREGOR: *(Quietly)* "YESTERDAY."
ERNA: "YESTERDAY. OH GOD WHEN I WOKE UP THIS MORNING AND SAW THE SUNSHINE—"
GREGOR: *(Pacing without looking at her)* SUNSHINE. SUNSHINE.
ERNA: "SUNSHINE, THAT GOLDEN LIGHT—"
GREGOR: *(Almost shouting now)* THAT GOLDEN LIGHT.
ERNA: "—AND SMELLED—"
GREGOR: SMELLED!!!
ERNA: "—SMELLED—"

GREGOR: *(Reading from his book)* "—SMELLED THE SPRING COMING. . . . "
ERNA: "—SMELLED THE SPRING COMING—"
GREGOR: "—IT MADE ME SO HAPPY . . . "
ERNA: "—IT MADE ME SO HAPPY—"
GREGOR: Say it right "—IT MADE ME SO HAPPY . . . "
ERNA: "—IT MADE ME SO HAPPY—." Gregor, I'm trying.
GREGOR: Then try harder.
ERNA: You mean as hard as you try?!
GREGOR: Once I want to hear it right—"—IT MADE ME SO HAPPY, I LONGED TO GO HOME."
ERNA: "—IT MADE ME SO HAPPY, I LONGED TO GO HOME."
GREGOR: Say it—"I LONG TO GO HOME." "I LONG TO GO HOME."!!!
ERNA: *(Screaming)* "I LONG TO GO HOME." "I LONG TO GO HOME." "I LONG TO GO HOME!!!!!"
(She throws her book at him. Long pause. ERNA *looks out the window.* GREGOR *looks away.)*
ERNA: *(More to herself than to* GREGOR, *she continues Olga's speech from* Three Sisters, *in Czech.)* "Every morning it's school, every afternoon and night there's tutoring. It's no wonder I get those headaches. I have started to think like an old woman. Really, after four years of this work—."
GREGOR: *(Quietly)* In English, Erna.
ERNA: "—it feels as if day after day all my strength, my youth is being drained out of me, squeezed, drop by drop. All that grows inside me now is that longing—"
GREGOR: In English!
ERNA: "—to go to Moscow! Sell the house, leave everything, and to Moscow!"

GREGOR: *(Screaming)*	ERNA: *(Shouting)*
In English!	To Moscow!
In English!	To Moscow!
In English!	To Moscow!

SCENE EIGHTEEN

Title:
THE CULMINATION ENDS

We are in the last few moments of Scene One.

ERNA: I'd better pack.
GREGOR: You'll come to Hartford? *(Pause.)* When?
ERNA: I'd better pack.
GREGOR: Come tomorrow. There's a train at ten. I'll make sure someone meets you. I'll talk to the stage manager. Erna . . . *(She has turned away.)*
GREGOR: It'll make us both feel better, I'm sure of it.
(He puts his coat on, goes to kiss her—she doesn't respond.)
ERNA: I'm glad you're sure of it.
GREGOR: *(At the door)* We'll go out to eat. What kind of food would you like? There's a very good Japanese restaurant near the theater. . . .
ERNA: Japanese? Yes. That would make sense for two Czechs in America.
(He goes. She turns the television back on.)
TELEVISION: "The opposition Social Democratic Party, ignoring an appeal by former Chancellor Helmut Schmidt, said today that it could not accept the deployment of American medium-range missiles in West Germany. The decision, taken at a special party congress in Cologne, was the culmination of—"
(The door opens; GREGOR *is in the doorway.)*
"—a left-wing rebellion against Mr. Schmidt's support for NATO's deployment decision, which contributed to the collapse of his government last year. A resolution adopted by the Social Democrats opposed the deployment of Pershing 2 and cruise missiles, demanded that the United States and the Soviet Union continue their deadlocked arms talks in Geneva, and called on the Soviet Union to reduce its armory of SS-20

missiles targeted on Western Europe. A two-way debate and a vote—"

(GREGOR *enters the room and turns off the television.*)

ERNA: *(Without looking at him)* Have you come back to give me the name of a good doctor?

(*She smiles to herself, gets up, and gets a cigarette. He shakes his head. Pause.*)

GREGOR: Why are we lying to each other?

ERNA: I haven't lied. I said I would pack—

GREGOR: *(Suddenly turns to her.)* Did they pay for your plane ticket? (*She nods. He takes out his wallet, opens it, and takes out a number of bills.*) Here—!

ERNA: *(Protesting)* Gregor—!

GREGOR: *(Throwing the money down, yells.)* Give it to your sister then!! *(Pause. He goes into the kitchen area, leans on the counter, and rubs his face.)* They pay me thirty-five dollars a day for meals. But I have sandwiches in my room. I bought a hot coil so I make my own coffee now in the morning.

ERNA: Aren't you smart to do that.

GREGOR: I'll make half my salary again that way.

ERNA: Not if you start throwing it away on women like my sister.

(*She looks at him, he turns away, shaking his head, trying not to smile.*)

GREGOR: You'll miss my interview. One of the Hartford papers wants to interview your husband, Erna. There will be a photo as well. *(Short pause.)* I could see if they'd use one of both of us.

ERNA: *(Disgusted)* Oh God, Gregor!

(*Pause.* GREGOR *rubs his eyes and sighs.*)

ERNA: You know you could still—

GREGOR: I know! I know, but . . .

(*Pause.*)

ERNA: Perhaps in time.

GREGOR: No. No. *(Short pause.)* Perhaps. *(Pause. Without looking up:)* They all call me just "Gregor." No one even asked. I like that. Even the black at the stage door calls me "Gregor." I'm treated . . . *(Looks up.)* That may seem like nothing to you—

ERNA: No. It doesn't seem like nothing to me.

(*Pause.*)

GREGOR: I will never look at another woman, Erna.

ERNA: *(Smiles.)* This is not the first time you have made me this promise.

GREGOR: When? When did I—?
ERNA: Sophia.
GREGOR: She meant nothing to me. I didn't marry her, Erna.
ERNA: No. No, you didn't. *(Pause. Realizing the time)* Gregor, the—!
GREGOR: I'll catch a later train.
(ERNA sits, GREGOR stands; they say nothing.)

SCENE NINETEEN

Title:
BETWEEN EAST AND WEST

GREGOR, *alone, sits watching television.*

TELEVISION: "The West German Bundestag, ignoring street demonstrations and warnings from Moscow, voted to proceed with the stationing of American-made, medium-range missiles.—"
(GREGOR stands and moves toward the television.)
"—When this was almost immediately followed by the arrival of the first nine of 108 Pershing 2's, Moscow broke off the negotiations in Geneva indefinitely, then announced its own deployment—"
(GREGOR turns the sound down. He goes to the phone.)
GREGOR: *(Into the phone)* I WISH TO MAKE A PHONE CALL TO PRAGUE, CZECHOSLOVAKIA, PLEASE. THANK YOU. *(Pause.)* YES. PRAGUE. CZECHOSLOVAKIA. THE NUMBER 86-491. 212-555-5312. THANK YOU.
(He hangs up. He goes into the kitchen and opens the refrigerator. He takes out a half-eaten McDonald's burger, a few leftover fries, and a half-empty shake. He sits back at the table. Opens them slowly, begins to eat. The phone rings.)
GREGOR: *(Into the phone)* HELLO? THANK YOU. . . . Hello, Erna? . . . Lucie. It is Gregor. I wish to speak to—. You don't know when she returns. What is she seeing? Oh.

Skreta's *Macbeth*. Tell her something for me . . . The critics did not like the production. No. They said it was too European. You are right. She will be very interested in that. Goodbye.
(He hangs up. Sits for a moment. Then goes and turns the television sound back on. And goes back to the table and eats without watching.)
TELEVISION: "—Accusing the United States of torpedoing the possibility of agreement in Geneva, the Soviet Union announced a further buildup of nuclear weapons in Czechoslovakia and East Germany as well as aboard submarines off the American coast. Whether intentional or not, the effect was to link the fate of Western Europe with that of the United States. Western leaders reacted calmly. The President said he regretted Moscow's attitude but professed confidence. 'I can't believe it will be permanent,' he said."

END